Her Majesty Queen Elizabeth The Queen Mother

The Life That Spanned a Century

1900-2002

SIDGWICK
&JACKSON

First published 2002 by Sidgwick & Jackson an imprint of Pan Macmillan Ltd
Pan Macmillan, 20 New Wharf Road, London N1 9RR Basingstoke and Oxford
Associated companies throughout the world www.panmacmillan.com

ISBN 0283 07369 1

Text by Margaret Laing   Editor James Bishop

1 3 5 7 9 8 6 4 2

A CIP catalogue record for this book is available from
the British Library.

Printed and bound in Great Britain by Butler & Tanner, Frome, Somerset.
A full list of photographs, credits and acknowledgements is given on page 130.

OUR GRACIOUS QUEEN MOTHER

The Queen Mother lived her life with such amazing grace and transparent joy that we can both mourn and celebrate its completion. Born in 1900, she grew up with the tumultuous 20th century, creating her own style for the roles she was destined to play: first as daughter-in-law to King George V and his formidable consort, next as sister-in-law to King Edward VIII, then as Queen, when her husband Bertie succeeded as King George VI, and as mother of the heir to the throne, and finally, for nearly half her life, as Queen Mother. And she died as she would have wished, peacefully in her sleep, well into the new millennium, which she was always determined to see in, and well past her own centenary.

Starting life as Elizabeth Angela Marguerite Bowes-Lyon, the ninth of ten children in a Scottish family, she became Lady Elizabeth at the age of four when her father succeeded to the earldom of Strathmore, and to Glamis Castle. She received what was then a conventional education for an aristocratic girl, being taught to read and write, to dance, sing, sew, knit and play, at home by her mother and a governess, quickly acquiring the social skills that stood her in good stead for the rest of her life.

She hesitated for some time when the Duke of York proposed to her, afraid of the public life that would lie ahead, but finally agreeing and devoting herself to supporting her husband, particularly when, as he had feared, "the worst happened" and his brother abdicated in order to marry Mrs Simpson. As Queen, friend, adviser and, as the King described her, "my helpmeet", Elizabeth fought to protect him, not just against the demands of the job but also against the threat of the continuing popularity of the Duke of Windsor.

The war brought out more of her fighting spirit, leading Hitler to declare that she was "the most dangerous woman in Europe". Buckingham Palace was bombed several times, prompting the Queen to say that she was glad of it, because it enabled her "to look the East End in the face". But undoubtedly her real service to the nation was the help and support she gave to her husband.

The Queen was only 51 when he died, and from that day in early February 1952 she had to fashion a new life for herself. There is no defined constitutional role for the widow of a British king, but her experience, her common sense, her charm, humour and her tact were assets too valuable to be lost. She was made a Counsellor of State and adopted a punishing load of royal engagements which she maintained beyond her hundredth birthday.

It is hard to appreciate the significance of a life that witnessed the changes brought about in the last century. As this publication recalls, they range from the relief of Mafeking, the first flight of a Zeppelin and the first transatlantic wireless message, through the mass production of the motor car, two world wars and the splitting of the atom, to men walking on the moon, the development of computer technology and instant communication. Through it all, this remarkable woman continued to make her presence felt and loved, bringing a gentle touch of gold to all she did.

VICTORIA'S LINE

Queen Victoria
by Winterhalter, 1859.

Prince Albert, the Prince
Consort, studio of Winterhalter.

VICTORIA
QUEEN VICTORIA
(1819-1901)
m
ALBERT
OF SAXE-COBURG & GOTHA
(1819-1861)

THOMAS LYON-BOWES
12th EARL OF STRATHMORE
(1822-1855)

CLAUDE LYON-BOWES
Changed name to Bowes-Lyon 13th EARL OF
STRATHMORE
(1824-1904)
m
FRANCES SMITH
(1833-1922)

VICTORIA
PRINCESS ROYAL
(1840-1901)
m
FREDERICK III
EMPEROR OF GERMANY
(1831-1888)

ALBERT
KING EDWARD VII
(1841-1910)
m
ALEXANDRA
OF DENMARK
(1844-1925)

ALICE
(1843-1878)
m
LUDWIG IV
GRAND DUKE OF HESSE-DARMSTADT
(1837-1892)

ALFRED
DUKE OF EDINBURGH AND SAXE-COBURG &
GOTHA
(1844-1900)
m
MARIE
OF RUSSIA
(1853-1920)

HELENA
(1846-1923)
m
CHRISTIAN
OF SCHLESWIG-HOLSTEIN
(1831-1917)

LOUISE
(1848-1939)
m
JOHN
DUKE OF ARGYLL
(1845-1914)

ARTHUR
DUKE OF CONNAUGHT
(1850-1942)
m
LOUISA
OF PRUSSIA
(1860-1917)

LEOPOLD
DUKE OF ALBANY
(1853-1884)
m
HELENA
OF WALDECK-PYRMONT
(1861-1922)

BEATRICE
(1857-1944)
m
HENRY
OF BATTENBERG
(1858-1896)

CLAUDE BOWES-LYON
14th EARL OF STRATHMORE
(1855-1944)
m
NINA CAVENDISH BENTINCK
(1862-1938)

6 SONS
3 DAUGHTERS

King Edward VII and Queen
Alexandra.

ALBERT
DUKE OF CLARENCE
(1864-1892)

GEORGE
KING GEORGE V
(1865-1936)
m
MARY
OF TECK
(1867-1953)

LOUISE
PRINCESS ROYAL
(1867-1931)
m
ALEXANDER
DUKE OF FIFE
(1849-1912)

VICTORIA
(1868-1935)

MAUD
(1869-1938)
m
HAAKON VII
KING OF NORWAY
(1872-1957)

Princes of Wales:
the future George V, above, and
Edward VIII, right.

VIOLET
(1882-1893)

MARY
(1883-1961)
m
SIDNEY
LORD ELPHINSTONE

PATRICK
15th EARL OF STRATHMORE
(1884-1949)
m
DOROTHY OSBORNE

JOHN
(1886-1930)
m
FENELLA HEPBURN-STUART-FORBES-
TREFUSIS

ALEXANDER
(1887-1911)

FERGUS
(1889-1915)
m
CHRISTIAN DAWSON-DAMER

ROSE
(1890-1967)
m
WILLIAM
LORD GRANVLLE

MICHAEL
(1893-1954)
m
ELIZABETH CATOR

ELIZABETH
QUEEN ELIZABETH THE QUEEN MOTHER
(1900-2002)
m
ALBERT
KING GEORGE VI
(1895-1952)

DAVID
(1902-1961)
m
RACHEL SPENDER-CLAY

EDWARD
KING EDWARD VIII
Abdicated 1936 became DUKE OF WINDSOR
(1894-1972)
m
WALLIS WARFIELD
(1896-1986)

ALBERT
KING GEORGE VI
(1895-1952)
m
ELIZABETH BOWES-LYON
QUEEN ELIZABETH THE QUEEN MOTHER
(1900-2002)

MARY
PRINCESS ROYAL
(1897-1965)
m
HENRY
EARL OF HAREWOOD
(1882-1947)

HENRY
DUKE OF GLOUCESTER
(1900-1974)
m
ALICE MONTAGU-DOUGLAS-SCOTT
(1901-   )

GEORGE
DUKE OF KENT
(1902-1942)
m
MARINA
OF GREECE
(1906-1968)

JOHN
(1905-1919)

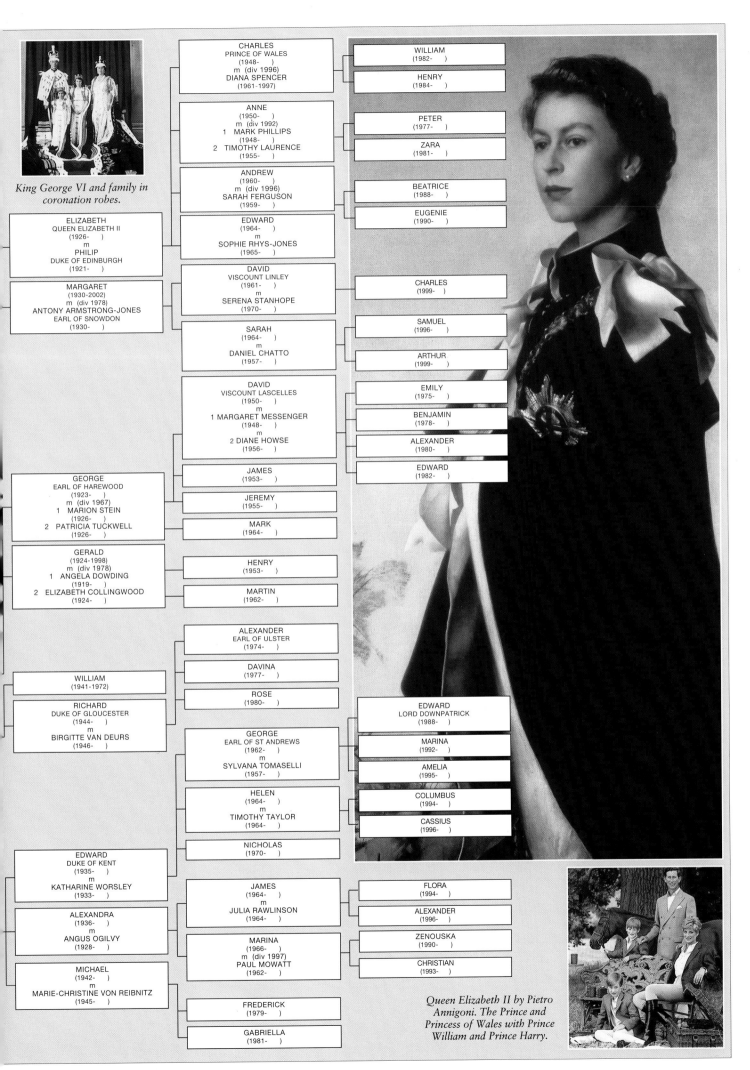

King George VI and family in coronation robes.

ELIZABETH
QUEEN ELIZABETH II
(1926-)
m
PHILIP
DUKE OF EDINBURGH
(1921-)

MARGARET
(1930-2002)
m (div 1978)
ANTONY ARMSTRONG-JONES
EARL OF SNOWDON
(1930-)

GEORGE
EARL OF HAREWOOD
(1923-)
m (div 1967)
1 MARION STEIN
(1926-)
2 PATRICIA TUCKWELL
(1926-)

GERALD
(1924-1998)
m (div 1978)
1 ANGELA DOWDING
(1919-)
2 ELIZABETH COLLINGWOOD
(1924-)

WILLIAM
(1941-1972)

RICHARD
DUKE OF GLOUCESTER
(1944-)
m
BIRGITTE VAN DEURS
(1946-)

EDWARD
DUKE OF KENT
(1935-)
m
KATHARINE WORSLEY
(1933-)

ALEXANDRA
(1936-)
m
ANGUS OGILVY
(1928-)

MICHAEL
(1942-)
m
MARIE-CHRISTINE VON REIBNITZ
(1945-)

CHARLES
PRINCE OF WALES
(1948-)
m (div 1996)
DIANA SPENCER
(1961-1997)

ANNE
(1950-)
m (div 1992)
1 MARK PHILLIPS
(1948-)
2 TIMOTHY LAURENCE
(1955-)

ANDREW
(1960-)
m (div 1996)
SARAH FERGUSON
(1959-)

EDWARD
(1964-)
m
SOPHIE RHYS-JONES
(1965-)

DAVID
VISCOUNT LINLEY
(1961-)
m
SERENA STANHOPE
(1970-)

SARAH
(1964-)
m
DANIEL CHATTO
(1957-)

DAVID
VISCOUNT LASCELLES
(1950-)
m
1 MARGARET MESSENGER
(1948-)
m
2 DIANE HOWSE
(1956-)

JAMES
(1953-)

JEREMY
(1955-)

MARK
(1964-)

HENRY
(1953-)

MARTIN
(1962-)

ALEXANDER
EARL OF ULSTER
(1974-)

DAVINA
(1977-)

ROSE
(1980-)

GEORGE
EARL OF ST ANDREWS
(1962-)
m
SYLVANA TOMASELLI
(1957-)

HELEN
(1964-)
m
TIMOTHY TAYLOR
(1964-)

NICHOLAS
(1970-)

JAMES
(1964-)
m
JULIA RAWLINSON
(1964-)

MARINA
(1966-)
m (div 1997)
PAUL MOWATT
(1962-)

FREDERICK
(1979-)

GABRIELLA
(1981-)

WILLIAM
(1982-)

HENRY
(1984-)

PETER
(1977-)

ZARA
(1981-)

BEATRICE
(1988-)

EUGENIE
(1990-)

CHARLES
(1999-)

SAMUEL
(1996-)

ARTHUR
(1999-)

EMILY
(1975-)

BENJAMIN
(1978-)

ALEXANDER
(1980-)

EDWARD
(1982-)

EDWARD
LORD DOWNPATRICK
(1988-)

MARINA
(1992-)

AMELIA
(1995-)

COLUMBUS
(1994-)

CASSIUS
(1996-)

FLORA
(1994-)

ALEXANDER
(1996-)

ZENOUSKA
(1990-)

CHRISTIAN
(1993-)

Queen Elizabeth II by Pietro Annigoni. The Prince and Princess of Wales with Prince William and Prince Harry.

7

Lady Elizabeth Bowes-Lyon
Mabel E. Hankey, 1908

CHAPTER 1

LADY ELIZABETH BOWES-LYON

Elizabeth Angela Marguerite Bowes-Lyon was born on August 4, 1900. The ninth of 10 children born to Lord and Lady Glamis, she was also the granddaughter of the 13th Earl of Strathmore who died when she was four. Her father then succeeded to the Strathmore title, to Glamis Castle and to £250,000, and she became Lady Elizabeth.

The first child of the family, Violet, had died before the ninth was born, leaving another daughter, Mary, as the eldest. Between her and Elizabeth came five sons and a daughter, Rose. Finally, in 1902, another son was born — David, who was to be Elizabeth's closest companion in childhood and her dearest friend until the end of his life in 1961.

Her surviving sisters, later Lady Elphinstone and Lady Granville, must have seemed more like aunts when she was very young, but they became close friends as she grew up and as the age gap (17 and 10 years respectively) that had made them mentors diminished in importance.

"Not so much a family as a clan" was a favourite description of the family. Their feeling for each other, and for their forbears, was very strong. In the 14th century King Robert II of Scotland, grandson of

Robert the Bruce, created the title of Lord Lyon for his son-in-law; and with the bride came her dowry of the royal hunting lodge of Glamis.

Money was added to rank by the marriage of the ninth Earl to Mary, the only daughter and heiress of the industrialist and member of Parliament, George Bowes. A southern address was also acquired in Hertfordshire, 30 miles from London: St Paul's Walden Bury, a gentle Georgian house, grown over with ivy and scented by honeysuckle. It was here that Elizabeth was born, and this house she regarded as her home.

Her nursemaid was Clara Knight, the sixth of 12 children of a farmer. Known as "Alah", because Clara was too difficult to pronounce, Mrs Knight found her charge "an easy, happy baby, crawling early, running at 13 months and speaking young". Apart from her mother, Elizabeth's closest companions at this time were the seven-year-old Michael, and Rose (already 11) — hardly playmates.

David's birth when Elizabeth was 20 months old gave her someone of her own to cherish — and to lead astray. "They were almost like twins", recollected one sister. "We were never separated if we could help it", agreed Sir David Bowes-Lyon later.

Elizabeth's own memories of childhood were set down some 20 years later: "At the bottom of the garden is the WOOD. There are carpets of primroses to sit on and her small brother David is always with her . . . Now it is time to go for haymaking, which means getting very hot in a delicious smell. Very often she gets up wonderfully early — about six o'clock — to feed her chickens and make sure they are safe after the dangers of the night. The chickens stubbornly insist on laying eggs in a place called the FLEA HOUSE, and this is where she and her brother go and hide from Nurse. Nothing is quite so good as the FLEA HOUSE, but the place called the HARNESS ROOM is very attractive too. Besides hens there are bantams, whose eggs-for-tea are so good."

Hiding from Nurse was a constant temptation because there were so many exciting things to do. Elizabeth loved animals and there were "dogs and tortoises, Persian kittens and 'Bobs', the Shetland pony . . . on wet days, the books that are best for reading in front of the fire, and a chest full of period custumes and wigs that went with their gorgeousness." Her love of dressing up was to prove a positive pleasure and asset all her life.

Although she was small for her age, and pale beneath her dark hair, she had a good appetite and a cook remembered regular raids made upon the kitchen by Elizabeth and David, raids in which Elizabeth "always took the lead". Her 20 months' seniority was doubtless the reason at first, but by the age of seven she had acquired something of a reputation for tact and social know-how. A friend of the family remembered that when, one day, a particularly difficult guest was expected and a conference was held to discuss procedure, one of her daughters exclaimed, "Let's ask Elizabeth. She can talk to *anyone*."

No doubt some memories have grown a good deal rosier with time but one contemporary witness was also keen-eyed. Lord Gorell described her as "responsive as a harp". Her skill at drawing others out, her more equal relationship with her brother when she was about 12 and he 10, and something of her view of life can clearly be seen in a conversation recorded by an artist, E. Gertrude Thomson, who was commissioned to paint her.

"Would you like to see David's and my garden?", she asked, and conducted Miss Thomson to it, not particularly large nor tidy, which contained a pool with a frog, proffered by David for her to stroke.

"'It's a very agreeable frog', I remarked.

"'And beautiful', said Elizabeth.

"'Most beautiful', said I.

"'It lives alone. It has no wife nor children', she added.

"'Perhaps it is a hermit?', I suggested.

"'Yes. It is a sort of hermit... Mother says that *you* live alone in your flat.'

"'I do.'"

Plainly both children thought this odd — no wonder in comparison with their own overflowing home — and David offered to give her the frog for company.

The next day Elizabeth sat for a portrait sketch — "an ideal sitter, scarcely moving her head and chatting delightfully".

"Do you believe in *ghosts*? . . . If you come to Glamis you will see *our* ghosts. We have *several* . . . I haven't seen them myself yet, but some day I may", all said, apparently, with a face wreathed in smiles.

It was at Glamis, where the family spent its holidays, that one long-standing family friend believes that Elizabeth's future sense of duty and responsibility may largely have been instilled into her. The relationship between the Earl and his retainers and tenants formed a complete social system, in which each honourably carried out his or her own responsibilities. "Brought up in these great Scottish castles, one saw all these people who were dependent upon one, and I think perhaps it made one less naughty than one might have been", remarked one observer, herself the daughter of a Scottish earl.

The chapel played an important part in the life of the massive castle and guests were expected to join in the daily family prayers there. Luncheon was organised on a vast scale — the family alone, without spouses, numbered 11, so with husbands and wives a family meal could number 20 and, with a few friends and neighbours and house-guests, it was not unusual for 50 to sit down for dinner. On special occasions pipers in Highland Dress marched round the table three times.

Lady Strathmore kept an excellent table and the Earl had a fine cellar. Elizabeth learnt from both, and was to become an excellent judge of both Burgundy and fine food.

When the skies were glowering Glamis could look gloomy indeed. But inside, the evenings were spent in the splendid family cosiness of the Great Hall with the wood burning in its 13-foot fireplace sending tongues of flame leaping up the chimney. Lady Strathmore or one of her daughters would play the piano while others sang ballads or songs; or everyone would play "The Game", their own version of charades. Both her love of fires and fireplaces and her enjoyment of charades were carried through Elizabeth's life into each of her palaces and homes.

Elizabeth's mother was in her late 30s when she was born, her father some 10 years older. "My father adored her . . . but it was really my mother who brought her up", said Lady Elphinstone.

Lord Strathmore was a conscientious landowner, a good sportsman and fundamentally a quiet, religious man. The Countess of Strathmore was equally religious, but more outgoing. One of her daughters described her to Dorothy Laird as "very talented, very go-ahead and so upright . . . she sewed lovely embroidery, which she designed herself. She had an extremely good ear for music, she would go to a concert . . . and come back and play it perfectly." She was also a keen gardener and had great zest for new occupations and ideas.

It was, however, her gaiety and understanding rather than her accomplishments that made her such a favourite. "She had a terrific sympathy: the young used to pour out their troubles to her and ask her for advice, often they would not go to their own parents." She was a skilful parent. "I never heard her say a harsh word in my life", said one of her daughters. "But we had to obey her, we knew that. We were brought up with very definite principles."

Lady Strathmore knew it was enough, when discovering that her youngest daughter had taken it into her head to re-design a pair of sheets with the aid of some scissors, simply to say "Elizabeth" in a very sad way. The culprit hung her head.

When David was born Lady Strathmore was 40 and she nick-named her two youngest children "My two Benjamins", with a nice mixture of biblical intimacy and personal humour. Many people, she joked, took them for her grand-children.

"My mother taught us to read and write", David wrote later. "At the ages of six and seven we could each of us have written a fairly detailed account of all the Bible stories. This was entirely due to our mother's teach-ings. She also taught us the rudiments of music, dancing and drawing, at all of which my sister became fairly proficient."

Professional music and dancing lessons came later. The Minister of Glamis, the Rev Stirton, remembered a tea-party after which Lady Strath-more sat at the piano and "two small figures seemed to rise from the floor and dance a quaint old minuet". It was Elizabeth, dancing in a long rose-pink hooped gown, and David, dressed as a jester complete with cap and bells. When Mr Stirton asked the girl who she was supposed to be, she replied "I call myself the Princess Elizabeth". He also noted her interest, at a very early age, in his portrait of Prince Charles — who had slept at the castle and left his watch ticking under his pillow as he fled his pursuers. Mr Stirton went on, "She very much wanted to go down into the burial vault of her ancestors, but I drew the line at that".

Governesses evoked a comment that revealed how early and firmly her mind could be made up: "Some governesses are nice", she wrote, "and some are not." Some were also French — enough to make her confident in the language, which would later prove to be a considerable asset.

When David was 10 and went away to school she revealed an unusual ability for so young a child to distinguish between her own feelings and those of others. "David went to school for the first time on Friday", she wrote to a friend, "I believe he is quite enjoying it. I miss him horribly." She and her mother continued to read a chapter of the Bible together each morning and then, as an experiment, she went for two terms to a day school in London. She won a prize for literature, but the school did not win her. Already capable of putting her small foot down, she declined to return for a third term.

It seemed likely that at school she missed the very close relationships she had at home, first with her brother, then her mother and that she also missed the adult life she had enjoyed in her various homes.

London itself was not strange to her. In 1904 her father had taken a lease on a Robert Adam house, 20 St James's Square. The family always spent the London season there, and David and Elizabeth played in the gardens in the square.

"You look pale", Elizabeth an-nounced one day to a footman. "Let's ask mother if you can come into the gardens with us. We have a key you know." The children had some exciting outings: "Once each year we were taken to the Drury Lane pantomime", David recalled, "where we sat enthralled from start to finish.

During the holidays my sister and I used to go to the theatre as often as we were allowed — usually to the cheaper seats as our purses never bulged." (She once telegraphed her father for extra funds "SOS".) "Eliza-beth had a wide taste in plays", continued her brother, "but I think Barrie's were her favourite."

In London, statesmen such as Lord Curzon and former Prime Minister Lord Rosebery were among the frequent political visitors to luncheon of which, unusually for a child at that time, Elizabeth was allowed to partake.

Then, on her 14th birthday, Eliza-beth's life changed completely. Her mother had taken a box at the Coliseum to celebrate. At 10.45 pm that night, war was declared on Germany. In the next few days four of her brothers enlisted: Patrick, John and Fergus in the Black Watch, and Michael in the Royal Scots. During the second week in August Elizabeth and her mother travelled to Glamis to organise the conversion of the castle into a hospital. Rose joined them after training as a nurse at a London hospital. In 1916 Rose married, as Mary had in 1910, leaving Elizabeth as the only daughter at home and, during term-time, the only child, since David was now at Eton.

Between the outbreak of war and 1919 more than 1,500 wounded men and officers stayed at Glamis. The tone was set on their arrival, when each one was greeted at the entrance by Lady Strathmore. Until her 18th birthday, Elizabeth spent four years not only, in her own words, "knitting, knitting, knitting", but also meeting and tending men of all types and from many parts of the UK and overseas whose personalities and backgrounds she could not previously have imagined. At a time when most girls are at their most romantic, she became a realist. She had always had a tendency to shrink from illness but now she was forced to overcome this. She found ways to distract the men from their mental suffering, listening to stories of home and loved ones, fetching tobacco, taking photographs they could send to their families — and on one occasion, when her snapshot had "cut off" a man's arm, hastily despatching another picture to the frantic parents as proof that he was intact.

A month after her 15th birthday Fergus was killed. Another brother, Alexander, had died in 1911. She had not been close enough to either to be overwhelmed by grief, but her mother was and so, for a time, it was Elizabeth who greeted newcomers and bade "farewell" to the convalescents ready to leave Glamis.

It was the first time Elizabeth had seen her mother really ill. And it was also the first time she had seen the horrors of suffering inflicted deliberately on man by man, and the effects of such pain on family life. In Lady Asquith's opinion it was the war that reinforced her sense of responsibility and, "explains why, at the age of 18, for all its gaiety the observant saw on her face a look of experience beyond her years".

Another strange experience had contributed to this. In 1917 her brother Michael was reported killed but David, refusing to wear mourning, declared he had seen him in a dream, his head bandaged and in a house surrounded by trees. This was later found to be true, but when he was to be repatriated, Michael had offered his place to another badly wounded man and the family did not see him again until 1919.

Elizabeth must have realised that there were more things in heaven and earth than she had dreamed of at her 14th birthday treat at the Coliseum. Her country had changed; so had she.

Chapter 2, Duchess of York, follows on page 27.

1900

Apr 24 *Daily Express* newspaper published for first time
May 17 Relief of Mafeking after 31 weeks' siege by the Boers
Jul 2 First flight of Zeppelin airship
Aug 4 Elizabeth Angela Marguerite Bowes-Lyon, youngest daughter of 14th Earl of Strathmore, born at St Paul's Walden Bury, Herts
Aug 8 First Davis Cup tennis tournament won by US
Aug 14 Siege of diplomatic legations in Peking, following Boxer uprisings, ended after 55 days
Sept 1 Transvaal annexed to British Empire
Oct 16 Conservative Government led by Lord Salisbury returned to power in "Khaki" election
Nov 30 Oscar Wilde died in exile in Paris, aged 43
Dec 22 Arthur Sullivan died, aged 58

1901

Jan 1 Commonwealth of Australia created from six colonies
Jan 22 Queen Victoria died, aged 81, after reigning for 63 years. Her 59-year-old son succeeded as Edward VII
Jan 27 Giuseppe Verdi died, aged 87
Aug 30 Vacuum cleaner patented by H.C. Booth
Sept 6 US President William McKinley shot. He died on Sept 14 and was succeeded by Theodore Roosevelt
Oct 2 First British submarine launched at Barrow
Dec 10 Nobel prizes instituted
Dec 12 First transatlantic wireless message transmitted by Marconi between Cornwall and Newfoundland

1902

Jan 17 *The Times Literary Supplement* published for first time
Jan 30 Anglo-Japanese Alliance ended Britain's "splendid isolation" in foreign policy
Mar 18 First phonograph recordings made by Italian tenor Enrico Caruso
Mar 26 Cecil Rhodes died, aged 49
May 2 Lady Elizabeth's younger brother David born
May 31 Boer War ended by Treaty of Vereeniging
Jun 23 The Order of Merit instituted
Aug 9 Edward VII gave Osborne House, Isle of Wight, to the nation

1903

May 5 Paul Gauguin died, aged 55
Jul 17 James Abbott McNeill Whistler died, aged 69
Aug 12 20mph speed limit for motorcars introduced
Nov 2 *Daily Mirror* first published
Dec 17 Wright brothers made first powered flight
Dec 18 US-Panama Treaty gave Canal Zone to US in perpetuity

Queen Victoria died on January 22, 1901. Her funeral was attended by the crowned heads of Europe including her grandson Kaiser Wilhelm II who rode in the funeral procession, right, with the new King of England.

The first powered flight was made by Wilbur and Orville Wright on December 17, 1903, at Kitty Hawk, North Carolina, USA.

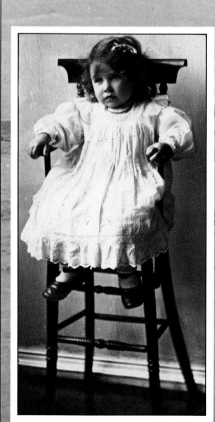

Lady Elizabeth Bowes-Lyon at the age of two.

The first of five British submarines, seen (right) passing the Victory *at Portsmouth, was launched at Barrow on October 2, 1901.*

1904 **Feb 4** Out-break of war between Russia and Japan
Apr 8 Anglo-French Entente settled outstanding colonial differences between the two countries
Jul 2 Anton Chekhov died, aged 44
Jul 19 First stone of Liverpool Cathedral laid
Dec 27 J. M. Barrie's *Peter Pan* first performed

1905 **Jan 22** Tsar's troops fired on demon-strators in front of Winter Palace in St Petersburg
Sept 5 Russo-Japanese war ended
Sept 26 Albert Einstein pub-lished paper on special theory of relativity
Oct 13 Sir Henry Irving died, aged 67
Nov 28 Sinn Fein founded in Dublin

1906 **Jan 12** Land-slide victory for Liberals in general election. First Lab-our MPs elected
Feb 10 Battleship HMS *Dread-nought* launched
Mar 10 Bakerloo tube line opened in London from Baker Street to Waterloo
Mar 16 Rolls-Royce founded
Apr 18 Two-thirds of San Francisco destroyed by earth-quake and fire
Oct 23 Paul Cézanne died, aged 66

1907 **Jul 29** Robert Baden-Powell organized experimental boys' camp from which Boy Scout movement was founded
Sept 26 New Zealand became a Dominion
Nov 16 Oklahoma became 46th American state

1908 **Feb 1** King Carlos I of Portugal and Crown Prince murdered in Lisbon
Mar 16 *The Times* bought by Lord Northcliffe
Apr 8 Prime Minister Henry Campbell-Bannerman resigned due to ill health (died Apr 22). He was succeeded by H. H. Asquith
Jul 21 Falkland Islands de-clared a British dependency
Nov 14 First Cubist exhibition, in Paris

1909 **Jan 1** First Government old-age pen-sions granted to people over 70
Mar 15 Selfridge's department store opened
Apr 6 US explorer Robert Peary became first man to reach North Pole
Apr 10 Algernon Charles Swinburne died, aged 72
Apr 29 David Lloyd George's "People's Budget" increased income tax and estate duty. Rejection by House of Lords led to constitutional crisis and dissolution of Parliament on Dec 2

Above, the first Labour MPs were returned to Parliament in the 1906 election. Pictured on the terrace of the House of Commons they included J Ramsay MacDonald, third from left, front row, and Keir Hardie, fifth from left, front row.

Right, Lady Elizabeth with her younger brother, David, in fancy dress at Glamis Castle, 1909.

Top, on April 18, 1906, much of the city of San Francisco, California, was destroyed by an earthquake and subsequent fire, making 250,000 people homeless. The Sphere carried pictures of the disaster, including this one of the ruined City Hall.

Centre, on February 10, 1906, the battleship Dreadnought was launched at Portsmouth. She was the first big-gun warship to be commissioned, having ten 12-inch guns in five turrets and a displacement of 21,845 tons.

Far left, the Scout movement grew from an experimental boys' camp held in July, 1907.

Left, in 1909 American Robert Peary leading an Arctic expedition became the first man to reach the North Pole.

17

Jul 25 Louis Blériot made first air crossing of Channel
Nov 5 First F.W. Woolworth store opened in Britain

1910
Jan 15 General election won by Liberals. Finance Bill was finally passed Apr 28
Feb 1 First Labour Exchanges opened
Apr 13 Florence Nightingale died, aged 90
May 6 Edward VII died, aged 68. He was succeeded by his 44-year-old second son as George V
May 31 Union of South Africa became a Dominion
Nov 10 Leo Tolstoy died, aged 82

1911
Feb 6 Ramsay MacDonald elected leader of British Labour Party
May 29 W.S. Gilbert died, aged 74
Aug 10 House of Lords passed Parliament Act curbing its own powers
Aug 10 House of Commons for first time voted salaries for MPs (£400pa)
Oct 4 First public escalator began operating at Earls Court underground station
Oct 26 China became republic following overthrow of Manchu dynasty
Dec 10 Marie Curie awarded Nobel Prize for the discovery of radium
Dec 12 King George V and Queen Mary held ceremonial Court at Delhi
Dec 15 The Norwegian Roald Amundsen reached South Pole

1912
Jan 1 General Post Office took over telephone systems
Jan 18 Robert Falcon Scott reached South Pole. He died with his companions during return journey
Jan 26 New Mexico became 47th American state
Feb 14 Arizona became 48th American state
Mar 26 Royal Flying Corps formed
Apr 15 The *Titanic* struck iceberg and sank in North Atlantic on maiden voyage. 1,513 of 2,224 passengers died
Jul 15 National Health Insurance Act came into force
Aug 20 William Booth, founder of Salvation Army, died aged 83
Sept 1 Samuel Coleridge-Taylor died, aged 37

1913
Jan 1 British Board of Film Censors began operating
Mar 18 George I of Greece assassinated after reign of nearly 50 years. He was succeeded by son, Constantine I
Apr 3 Emmeline Pankhurst sentenced to three years' penal servitude for inciting persons to place explosives outside Lloyd George's house. She was released after one year
Apr 12 *New Statesman*

Above, the liner Titanic *struck an iceberg in the North Atlantic on April 15, 1912, during her maiden voyage and went down with the loss of 1,513 lives.*

Right, Lady Elizabeth at 14, photographed by E D Hoppe.

Far right, the Royal Flying Corps was formed on March 26, 1912, and merged with Royal Naval Air Service in 1918 as the Royal Air Force.

founded by Sidney and Beatrice Webb

Jun 4 Suffragette Emily Davison threw herself in front of the King's horse in the Derby

Jul 1 Zanzibar was incorporated with British East Africa

Oct 7 Henry Ford introduced first car production line in USA

1914

Jun 28 Archduke Franz-Ferdinand of Austria and his wife assassinated in Serbia

Jul 25 W.G. Grace played his last game of cricket

Jul 28 Austria-Hungary declared war on Serbia

Aug 1 Germany declared war on Russia

Aug 3 Germany declared war on France and invaded Belgium

Aug 4 Britain declared war on Germany

Aug 7 First British troops arrived in France

Aug 15 First Vessel, *Ancón*, passed through the Panama Canal

Sept 15 Irish Home Rule Bill suspended for duration of war

Oct 30-Nov 24 Battle of Ypres set pattern of trench warfare

Nov 14 Lord Roberts died of pneumonia on visit to front, aged 82

1915

Jan 19 German airships bombed East Anglian ports

Feb 18 German U-boat blockade of Britain began

Mar 18 Assault on Dardanelles began

Apr 22-May 25 Second Battle of Ypres. Poison gas used for first time

May 4 Italy joined war against Germany

May 7 British liner *Lusitania* sunk by German U-boat. 1,198 of 1,959 passengers died

May 25 Liberal-Conservative coalition formed with Asquith Prime Minister

Sept 11 Women's Institute established in Britain

Oct 12 Edith Cavell executed by German firing squad in Brussels

1916

Jan 27 Compulsory Military Service Act passed

Feb 21-Dec 16 Battle of Verdun

Feb 28 Henry James died, aged 72

Apr 24-30 Easter rising of Sinn Fein in Dublin suppressed by British troops

May 21 Summer Time (daylight saving) introduced

May 31-Jun 1 Battle of Jutland

Jun 5 Lord Kitchener killed when HMS *Hampshire* sunk by mine off Orkneys

Jul 1-Nov 8 Battle of the Somme

Sept 15 Tanks used by British for first time

Dec 30 Rasputin, Siberian peasant whose great influence in Russian Court made him many enemies, was murdered

Left, Archduke Franz Ferdinand of Austria and his wife were assassinated at Sarajevo moments after this picture was taken on June 28, 1914, an event which led to Austria declaring war on Serbia on July 28 and ultimately to the outbreak of the First World War.

Tanks were used by the British for the first time on September 15, 1916.

Bottom, Tsar Nicholas II of Russia with his family. He abdicated on March 16, 1917, and the family was killed by the Bolsheviks on July 16.

Left, W. G. Grace played his last game of cricket on July 25, 1914. He was 66 years old, had scored 54,896 runs including 126 centuries in first-class cricket and as a bowler took 2,876 wickets.

Above, Lady Elizabeth says goodbye to a soldier who has been convalescing at Glamis during the First World War.

1917

Mar 16 Tsar Nicholas II of Russia abdicated

Apr 6 US declared war on Germany

Jun 22 George V instituted the Order of the British Empire and the Order of the Companions of Honour

Jul 17 Royal family abandoned German titles and assumed surname of Windsor

Jul 31-Nov 10 Battle of Passchendaele

Sept 26 Edgar Degas died

Sept 29 German aircraft bombed London

Oct 15 Mata Hari shot as German spy

Nov 2 Balfour Declaration pledged British Government to establishment of national home for Jews in Palestine

Nov 6 Bolshevik revolution began in Petrograd. Lenin became head of new government

Nov 17 Francois Auguste Rodin died, aged 77

1918

Feb 10 Russia ended state of war with Germany

Feb 16 British Electoral Reform Act extended suffrage to 8 million new voters, including women over 30

Apr 1 Royal Air Force formed

Apr 21 German flying ace the "Red Baron" shot down and killed

Jul 16 Tsar Nicholas II and family executed by Bolsheviks

Aug 8 Education Act provided for free and compulsory education for children aged 5 to 14

Nov 8 Kaiser abdicated; hostilities ceased on Western Front

Nov 11 Armistice signed

1919

Jan 18 Versailles Peace Conference opened. Treaty, signed on June 28, included establishment of League of Nations

Apr 10 During anti-British demonstrations at Amritsar, India, troops fired on unarmed mob

Jun 1 Ernest Rutherford published his findings on splitting of the atom

Jun 14-15 RAF officers Captain Alcock and Lieutenant Whitten-Brown made first non-stop transatlantic flight in 16 hours 27 minutes

Sept 1 First regular air service between London and Paris

Nov 28 Lady Astor became first woman MP

Dec 3 Pierre Auguste Renoir died, aged 78

1920

Jan 16 First meeting of Council of League of Nations

Jan 17 Prohibition of alcoholic liquor came into force in US

Apr 25 Palestine established as Jewish State under British administration

Apr 30 Conscription abolished in UK

May 15 British reinforcements sent to Ireland in face of con-

Left, the King and Queen drove through the celebrating crowds in Trafalgar Square after the Armistice ending the First World War was signed on November 11.

Above, Lady Astor being sworn in at the House of Commons after being elected as Britain's first woman MP in November 1919.

Right, Lady Elizabeth Bowes-Lyon pictured with her father, the Earl of Strathmore.

tinued agitation

Jul 23 Kenya became a Crown Colony

Oct 7 First women admitted to Oxford University

1921

Mar 17 Marie Stopes opened Mothers' Clinic for Constructive Birth Control

Mar 31 Gordon Richards, riding *Gay Lord* in an apprentice race at Leicester, rode first of his 4,870 winners

May 21 British Legion for War Veterans formed

Jul 22 *Chu-Chin-Chow* ended run of nearly 5 years

Sept 11 Lord Milford Haven, known until 1917 as Prince Louis of Battenberg, died aged 67

Dec 6 Treaty with Ireland established Irish Free State with Dominion status. Northern Ireland given option of separate existence

1922

Jan 5 Sir Ernest Shackleton died at sea off South Georgia, aged 48

Feb 15 International Court of Justice held first sessions at The Hague

Feb 28 Princess Mary, only daughter of George V, married Viscount Lascelles

Mar 15 British protectorate in Egypt ended. Sudan came under joint Anglo-Egyptian sovereignty

Mar 18 Gandhi sentenced to six years' imprisonment for civil disobedience

Aug 1 Alexander Graham Bell died, aged 75

Oct 28 Benito Mussolini's black shirts marched on Rome and he was established as dictator in Italy

Nov 14 British Broadcasting began "2LO" broadcasts from Marconi House, Strand

Nov 26 Howard Carter discovered Tutankhamun's tomb

Dec 6 Irish Free State officially proclaimed. Northern Ireland voted for non-inclusion on Dec 7

1923

Jan 1 Russia became the Union of Soviet Socialist Republics

Jan 16 Engagement of Duke of York and Lady Elizabeth Bowes-Lyon

Mar 3 *Time* first published

Mar 26 Sarah Bernhardt died, aged 77

Apr 26 Duke of York and Lady Elizabeth Bowes-Lyon married in Westminster Abbey

May 26 Transjordan became autonomous state

Aug 11 First Wightman Cup tennis tournament won by Americans

Aug 13 Turkey proclaimed a republic

Sept 1 Tokyo and Yokohama destroyed by earthquake

Sept 28 *Radio Times* first published

Royal tours: The Duke and Duchess of York visited Yugoslavia

Lady Elizabeth Bowes-Lyon married Albert, Duke of York, on April 26, 1923. Above left, she left her parents' house in Bruton Street for Westminster Abbey. Her dress, left, was of chiffon moiré with a natural waistline rather than the dropped waistline fashionable at the time.

Above, after the ceremony the Duke and Duchess of York were pictured with their parents, the Earl and Countess of Strathmore and King George V and Queen Mary.

Right, the couple left the Palace for their honeymoon which was spent at Polesden Lacey, Surrey, far right.

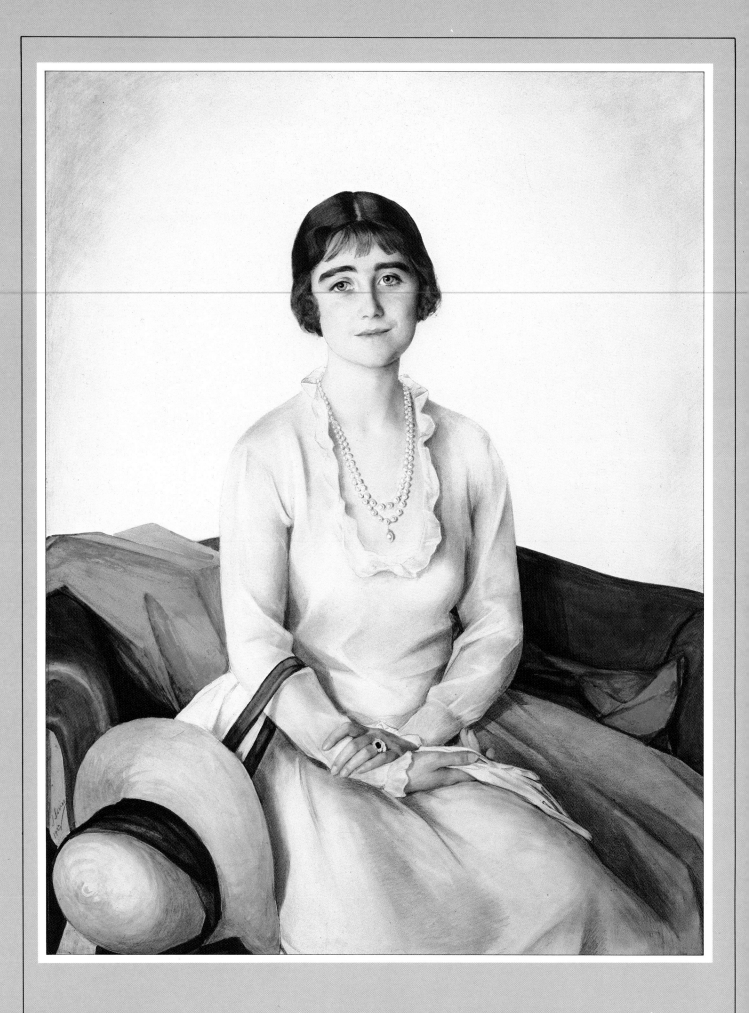

The Duchess of York
Savely Sorine, 1923

CHAPTER 2

THE DUCHESS OF YORK

In the spring of 1921 Prince Albert ("Bertie"), Duke of York, second son of King George and Queen Mary, told his parents that he intended to propose to Lady Elizabeth Bowes-Lyon. The King's opinion of both his son and his hoped-for bride can be gauged from his brief rejoinder: "You will be a lucky fellow if she accepts you."

The Duke later said that he had fallen in love, without fully realising it, when he had seen Lady Elizabeth at a dance given in May, 1920, by Lord and Lady Farquhar at their London home in Grosvenor Square. But this was not the first time he had met her. When Elizabeth was five and Bertie 10 she had been driven from St James's Square to a children's tea party at Montague House, and is said to have given the cherries from the top of her cake to the thin young prince sitting next to her. Through the Girl Guides she had also become a friend of Princess Mary, Bertie's younger sister, who gave informal dances in her rooms at Buckingham Palace.

A friend of the Strathmores thinks that Princess Mary may have been encouraged to invite her lively half-Scottish friend because "both she and David [the Prince of Wales] had high spirits, and I think it was thought they might get on well together". The King and Queen had been suffering agonies of anxiety about the future of the eldest of their four sons and of the throne. David was known by high society to be "rather in love" with Mrs Dudley Ward, "a pretty little fluff", but evidently not the stuff of which royal brides should be made.

The Prince of Wales, 18 months older than Bertie, had always outshone him in effervescence, confidence — he even argued with his father — and looks. "Too small, but really a pretty face", commented Lady Asquith.

The King, supported by Queen Mary, ran his home on such strict lines that the love they felt for their children was shown not in terms of affection or encouragement, but of admonishments and commands often sent by letter.

On Bertie's fifth birthday he received a missive from his father that read, "Now that you are five years old, I hope that you will always try to be obedient and to do at once what you are told, as you will find it will come to you much easier the earlier you begin." Six years later he wrote, "You really must give up losing your temper when you make a mistake — remember you are nearly 12 years old." How different from Lady Strathmore's one word reproach, "Elizabeth!"

And how much less productive. Nor was there help at hand. The children's nurse was sadistic, and irregular meals upset the nervous Bertie's digestion. Like most of the York children he had knock-knees and for long periods was forced to wear splints "to straighten them"; sometimes these were kept on at night too. The arrival of a tutor who forced the naturally left-handed child to write with his right hand only added to the problems and may have been responsible for the stammer he developed at about the age of eight. This made the pronunciation of English, let alone French and the family's second tongue, German, almost impossible.

So a sensitive, highly-conscientious and anxious-to-please Bertie grew up aware that his parents looked down on him and his stammer. His frustrated efforts to express himself sometimes vented themselves in a temper that revealed a sterner side: one that would prove his saviour in the moulding hands of Elizabeth.

At 13 he entered the Royal Naval College of Osborne — a gruelling experience for a boy who had never left home before and had the dual disadvantages of royal rank and a deep-seated sense of inferiority. He passed out bottom; but his college Captain noted, "He shows the grit and 'Never say I'm beaten spirit' which is strong in him." Bertie went on to Dartmouth and then into the Navy where he was on the battleship *Collingwood* during the Battle of Jutland, after which his Captain wrote, "Prince Albert was in bed on the sick list when we prepared for action but got up and went to his turret, where he remained until we finally secured guns next day."

It was the gastric troubles, first noticed in childhood, that put him on the sick list before the battle; soon they forced his resignation from the Navy and, in 1917, an operation. Not one to give up, however, Bertie became, in 1919, the first member of the Royal Family to qualify as a pilot. He also loved hunting, was a good shot and, surprisingly after the splints, a good athlete and tennis player. In this his frequent partner was his lifelong friend Louis Greig, with whom he spent two terms at Cambridge in the autumn of 1920 and spring of 1921. Greig said, "My principal contribution was to put steel into him"; but iron was already there to be tempered.

With such a hard life and struggle behind him, perhaps it is not surprising that he did not give up when Elizabeth refused his proposal of marriage. Besides, he had many allies, some of them in surprising places. Mabell, Countess of Airlie, an old friend of Queen Mary's (and grandmother of Angus Ogilvie who was to marry Bertie's niece, Princess Alexandra) wrote: "When I was driving with her one afternoon in the winter of 1920 she told me that the Prime Minister [Lloyd George] had advised the King that the country would not tolerate an alliance with a foreigner for the Prince of Wales and that the Duke of York should also look for a bride among the British aristocracy. 'I don't think Bertie will be sorry to hear that,' the Queen added, 'I have discovered that he is very much attracted to Lady Elizabeth Bowes-Lyon. He's always talking about her. She seems a charming girl, but I don't know her well.' I replied that I had known her all her life and could say nothing but good of her."

Even before he proposed the Duke had begun to ask Lady Airlie's advice on courtship procedure. Elizabeth, who certainly realised the question was coming, had done the same. Now, said Lady Airlie, they "started dropping in at my flat, on various pretexts, always separately, but each talked of the other. She was frankly doubtful, uncertain of her feelings and afraid of the public life that would lie ahead of her as the King's daughter-in-law. He was deeply in love but so humble".

So humble — but so determined.

Lady Elizabeth was said to have "taken London by storm". Since, despite the loveliness of her lambent, blue eyes, her complexion and sweet expression, she was no raving beauty and dressed, it seemed, deliberately unfashionably (Lord David Cecil described her style as "picturesque"), it was clearly her character and personality that won admiration. One male praised such contrasting qualities as her "unruffled serenity" and "great love of argument", together with an ability to express opinions very trenchantly — a talent which she would have in future to learn to reserve for private occasions.

She held her five feet two inches very erect, moved lightly, a little like a dancer, and had learnt from her mother "never look at your feet". But her chief talent seems still to have been that remarked upon by her childhood friends — to change the mood by finding a topic on which the shy longed, and were able, to elaborate; to turn aside an awkward moment with a *non sequitur* or a laugh, sometimes at a pre-planned signal from a conspirator.

If, as Lady Airlie said, "Her radiant vitality and a blending of gaiety, kindness and sincerity made her irresistible to men", she had not, it seemed, met anyone irresistible to her. This must have been a most alarming realisation for someone of whom it was said: "One knew instinctively that she was a girl who would find real happiness only in marriage and motherhood. A born homemaker."

There was considerable disappointment in both families when the Duke was turned down, and Lady Strathmore wrote, "I do hope he will find a nice wife who will make him happy. I like him so much and he is a man who will be made or marred by his wife..." The Strathmore prescience was echoed by Queen Mary who thought, "this was the one girl who could make Bertie happy", but resolved to say nothing to either of them. "Mothers should never meddle in their children's love affairs."

Spoken or silent, a formidable array of support was drawn up in favour of the Duke, whatever the 20-year-old Elizabeth's doubts.

Passionately loyal to family, country and ideals, it is less easy to picture her as passionate in romance. She had seen too many men — father, brothers, soldiers — stripped of glamour. Quick to feel, she could be very slow indeed to decide and to act. The marriage offered security even at a time when thrones were becoming shakier. It would also thrust many extra responsibilities upon her. She was already used to many of these and in sympathy with the extra duties she would have to take on, so it was not *a* royal marriage but *this* royal marriage that probably deterred her. The King was so strict that his own sons feared him; she would lose the freedom she loved and the privacy.

All this turned over in her mind for nearly two years while Queen Mary, in spite of her resolve not to meddle, took Bertie and his sister Mary with her up to Scotland to visit Lady Airlie and engineered an invitation to Glamis — where she was much impressed by Elizabeth's knowledge of Scottish history.

Bertie wrote "It is delightful here and Elizabeth is very kind to me." In a revealing phrase, he added, "The more I see her the more I like her."

A repeat visit was organised in September, 1922, and afterwards Lady Strathmore wrote: "That winter [1922-23] was the first time I have ever known Elizabeth really worried. I think she was torn between her longing to make Bertie happy and her reluctance to take on the big responsibilities which this marriage must bring." Perhaps, in the end, it was the knowledge that she, more than anyone else, could help Bertie that tipped the balance. Her mother had taken the family lead at home. Elizabeth herself had always enjoyed the bliss of inseparably close relationships. She needed to be needed; and no one could offer her more in emotional reward, as well as security, in this way.

So, on January 13, when the Duke of York again proposed to Lady Elizabeth at St Paul's Walden Bury she accepted. She commented later, "I am not sure that of the two of us I wasn't the more surprised."

The Duke telegraphed a coded message, "ALL RIGHT BERTIE", to his parents, and to Lady Airlie he wrote, "my dream... has at last been realised... It seems too marvellous to me that my darling Elizabeth will one day be my wife." Here was fully revealed the passionate strength and sweetness of a man filled with radiant optimism: but however well he could express himself in writing, he remained inhibited in speech and confidence.

The practical impediments to the marriage were overcome by a special Act of Parliament sanctioning the Duke's marriage to a commoner and the wedding took place on April 26, 1923, when she was 22 and he 27. The religious significance of the ceremony was deeply felt by both.

The King, who shortly before had pontificated on daughters-in-law — "I must say I dread the idea and always have" — now admitted, "She is a pretty and charming girl", to which Queen Mary added "engaging and natural" and David admitted the hitherto unmentionable, "She brought a lively and refreshing spirit to family life." Life had never been that before, either at Buckingham Palace, where the King and Queen wore full evening dress — and she a tiara — even when they dined alone; at Sandringham, where the clocks were 30 minutes fast to ensure an early start to a day's shooting; at Windsor, where a special uniform was worn by the male members of the Royal Family and senior members of their Household; or in any of their other homes, ruled to a precision that an Olympic skier would envy, by fractions of a second.

Some glimmer of the bride's aura was reflected in the King's pronouncement when she arrived late at the table — and one can imagine her husband's dread, then incredulity, on hearing: "You are not late my dear; we must have sat down two minutes early." Even so she did not dare protest to her father-in-law when they were given Royal Lodge in Richmond Park as their abode — old-fashioned, neglected and, above all, inconvenient both for their official duties and their private life in London. She became, remembers a confidante, "good at borrowing bedrooms", and no one knew when they stayed at her parents' new home at 17 Bruton Street.

Weekends were often spent at or near St Paul's Waldenbury, the new Duchess of York with her family while the Duke perhaps hunted during the day. She did not hunt but sometimes followed by car. Duff Cooper wrote after seeing them at a theatre, "They are such a sweet little couple and so fond of each other."

Yet over the Duke's head, and in spite of all the wife's soothing serenity and encouragement, her gaiety and her expressed confidence in him, hung his belief that his parents still held him in low regard. After three years of marriage the Duchess finally persuaded him to try the seemingly impossible once more and seek help with his speech problem from an Australian therapist, Lionel Logue.

Logue saw in his patient "a slim, quiet man with tired eyes" and thought he was suffering from melancholia or depression. Anyone who has known someone in this condition must realise that the Duchess had won the hardest battle by persuading her husband to go to Logue's consulting rooms.

Daily hours of practice followed. Then came the final horror of speaking in public: yet while the Duke suffered and struggled the Duchess sat, gloved hands calmly in her lap, smiling confidently — an actress who inspired courage in the protagonist and patience in his audience.

The Duchess had shone abroad on brief trips to Yugoslavia ("entrancing", pronounced Queen Marie of Rumania); to Northern Ireland: "She knows exactly what to do and say to all the people we meet", wrote Bertie to his father; and on a five-week safari to Africa, which she loved and where she showed her proficiency with a rifle.

On April 21, 1926, almost exactly three years since they had married, Princess Elizabeth was born at the home of the Duchess's parents. The birth was by Caesarian section but the Duchess's love of privacy inspired the bulletin that "a certain line of treatment" was taken. Since the Prince of Wales was still expected to marry and produce an heir the baby's arrival was not recognised as being of the very greatest constitutional importance. Lady Airlie recalled that when she had called to see her, "I little thought I was paying homage to the future Queen of England."

"I'm so proud of Elizabeth after all she has gone through in these last few days", recorded Bertie — for a difficult birth had been foreseen. The Duchess wrote of her baby later: "It almost frightens me that people should love her so much." One of the penalties of royalty was the ability to arouse powerful emotions that were not always predictable.

A more immediate penalty was having to leave her baby behind, aged only eight-and-a-half months, while she accompanied the Duke on a six-month tour of Australia and New Zealand. Her reward for this painful deprivation was immense, and came about in an unexpected way. Bertie was as thrilled by, and proud of, his wife's ability to charm strangers in the Dominions as in Britain, but when she was struck down with tonsilitis he dreaded going on alone.

Persuaded to do so, he telephoned her each evening with the day's news. After a visit to Christchurch he must have sounded unusually excited for it was, in the words of an eye-witness, his reception "there and in Dunedin which opened the Duke of York's eyes to his popularity. I really believe that in his humble way he thought no one would bother to turn out to see him alone, and when the streets were crowded with enthusiastic, happy people . . . he was quite overwhelmed and from that moment grew in confidence and stature."

Returning to London, the Duke and Duchess found 14-month-old Princess Elizabeth — who had been "shared" in their absence by the Strathmores and her royal grandparents — already able to say a few words, and installed in what was to be the Yorks' London address for nearly 10 years. This was 145 Piccadilly, a four-storey terrace house which they felt was the first real home of their own. It had been renovated for them and had an innovation insisted upon by the Duchess — double glazing.

They made the most of this private home, enjoying many evenings there when public duties did not call. The Duchess would read and play patience. The Duke, an expert embroiderer, made a dozen chair covers in *petit point* which later adorned seats in their country residence at Windsor, The Royal Lodge. Quite often they would slip out unnoticed to the cinema or, noticed, to the theatre.

On August 21, 1930 — the year the Duke of Windsor met Mrs Simpson — the Duchess gave birth to her second child, Princess Margaret Rose, at Glamis. It was the last accouchement at which the Home Secretary's presence was required as an official witness. The succession was a rising thought in the minds of Ministers and perhaps of the nation. "Lilibet", as Princess Elizabeth called herself, looked a more likely heir presumptive with the passing of each day.

The Duchess was determined that her daughters' lives should follow the pattern of her own happy childhood. So each day began with "high jinks" in their parents' bedroom, "no matter how busy the day, how early the start", and the Duchess enjoyed playing hopscotch and Racing Demon with them before the regular evening bathtime romp.

King George V and Queen Mary celebrated the Silver Jubilee of their reign on May 6, 1935. Increasingly despairing about his eldest son and Mrs Simpson, the King confided to a friend, "I pray to God my eldest son will never marry and that nothing will come between Bertie and Lilibet and the throne."

That winter both the Duchess and her father-in-law fell ill. Her influenza led to pneumonia, and while she lay weak in bed the news came that the King was dying. Afterwards the Duchess admitted to her doctor, "I miss him dreadfully... He never spoke one unkind or abrupt word to me, and was always ready to listen and give advice on one's own silly little affairs. He was so kind, and so *dependable*."

In the following spring, with very little warning, David, now King Edward VIII, brought Mrs Simpson to tea at the Royal Lodge. Miss Crawford, Lilibet's governess, afterwards revealed, "She had a distinctly proprietary way of speaking to the new King. I remember she drew him to a window and suggested how certain trees might be moved and a part of a hill taken away to improve the view. I have never admired the Duke and Duchess more than on that afternoon. They made the best of this awkward occasion and gave no sign whatever of their feelings." This must have taken superhuman control. The Royal Lodge was their favourite home and the Duke himself had created much of the garden, clearing undergrowth and planting with the aid of his family and anyone else who volunteered.

Some unforeseen changes had already taken place. The new King had dismissed old retainers from Balmoral without consulting or even informing Bertie, to the latter's great distress, and his carelessness with despatch boxes was becoming legendary. "Nor can any man control him", said Baldwin, the Prime Minister.

The young Duke of Kent summed up his brother's feeling for Mrs Simpson as "besotted" and, as the threat of abdication mounted, Bertie wrote to his mother, "It is all so worrying and I feel we all live a life of conjecture, never knowing what will happen." As the crisis deepened the Duchess again succumbed to influenza — she seldom outwardly showed worry but illness did seem to coincide with anxiety in her life — and it was in the Duchess's sickroom that a former and a future Queen Consort met and tried to console each other as the Abdication was decided upon.

The Duchess said to her daughter's governess, "I'm afraid there are going to be great changes in our lives, Crawfie. We must all take what is coming to us and make the best of it."

Religion was still strong in her marriage and her life. To the Archbishop of Canterbury she later admitted, "The strange thing was, we were not afraid."

Chapter 3, Queen Elizabeth, follows on page 40.

1924

Jan 10 Submarine L24 sank after collision with dreadnought *Resolution* off Portland
Jan 21 Lenin died, aged 53. Stalin and Trotsky took power
Jan 22 First Labour Government took office under Ramsay MacDonald
Mar 1 Vehicles allowed to drive through Hyde Park for first time
Oct 29 Labour Government defeated by Conservatives under Stanley Baldwin
Nov 2 First crossword in British newspaper (*Sunday Express*)
Royal tours: Duke and Duchess of York paid official visits to Northern Ireland; East Africa and Sudan

1925

Mar 18 Madame Tussaud's waxwork collection destroyed by fire
Apr 28 Britain returned to Gold Standard
May 1 Cyprus became a Crown Colony
Nov 20 Queen Alexandra, widow of Edward VII, died aged 80

1926

Jan 27 Television given first public demonstration in London by inventor John Logie Baird
Mar 6 Shakespeare Memorial Theatre, Stratford-upon-Avon, destroyed by fire
Apr 21 A daughter, Elizabeth Alexandra May, born to the Duchess of York
May 1 Coal miners went on strike refusing to accept pay cut and to work extra hour a day
May 4 Three million workers in Britain responded to General Strike in support of miners. Volunteers maintained essential services until strike ended on May 12
May 9 Richard Byrd became first man to fly over North Pole
Jul 26 Roundabout system of traffic control introduced at Piccadilly Circus
Aug 23 Rudolf Valentino died, aged 31
Oct 23 Trotsky expelled from Politbureau. Stalin established as virtual dictator of USSR
Nov 19 Miners returned to work

1927

Jan 1 British Broadcasting Company nationalized as British Broadcasting Corporation, with Sir John Reith as Director-General
Jan 7 Transatlantic telephone service inaugurated
May 20-21 Charles Lindbergh became first man to make solo flight across Atlantic
Jun 5 First Ryder Cup golf tournament won by America
Jun 20 Greyhound racing began at White City
Oct 6 *The Jazz Singer*, first talkie, opened in New York
Nov 12 First automatic tele-

The Duchess of York rapidly became a popular guest at public occasions. Left, she distributed gifts at an Elizabethan fete at Hatfield. Above, she and the Duke visited the Empire exhibition at Wembley in 1925.

Left, the Yorks' first child, Elizabeth Alexandra May, was born on April 21, 1926.

Above, on May 4, 1926, three million workers responded to a general strike in support of coal miners who had gone on strike on May 1, having refused to accept a pay cut and to work an extra hour a day. The General Strike ended on May 12, but the miners did not go back to work until November 19.

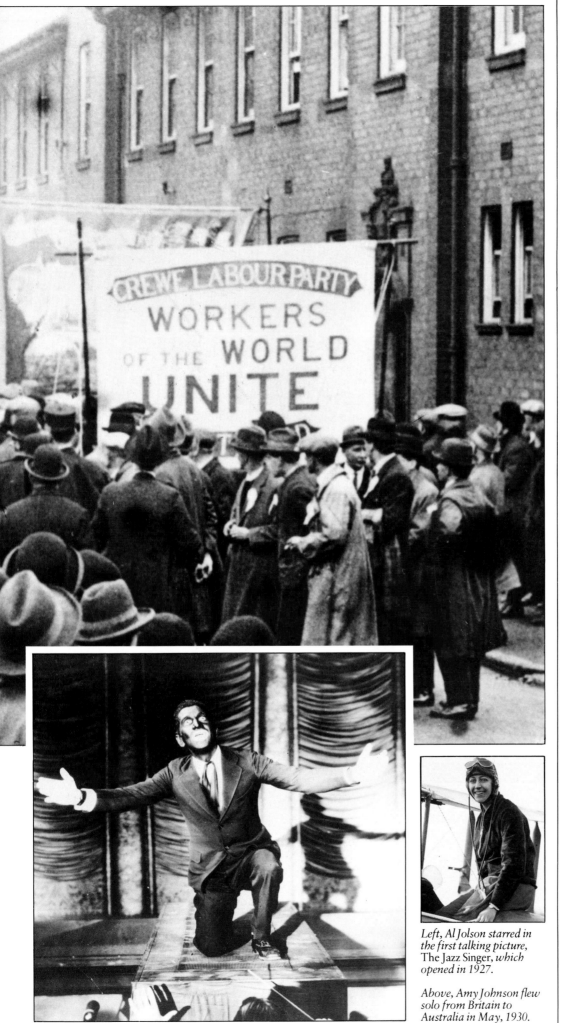

phone service in London inaugurated at Holborn

Royal tours: The Duke and Duchess of York visited Australia and New Zealand, Jamaica, Mauritius, Malta, Gibraltar

1928 Jan 11 Thomas Hardy died, aged 87
Jan 13 War Office abolished lance as weapon of war
Feb 11 Traffic lights introduced in UK
Apr 19 *Oxford English Dictionary* completed
May 7 Age limit for women's suffrage reduced to 21 years
Jun 14 Emmeline Pankhurst died, aged 69
Jul 21 Dame Ellen Terry died, aged 80
Sept 20 Alexander Fleming discovered antibacterial properties of penicillin

1929 Feb 14 St Valentine's Day gangland massacre in Chicago
Feb 16 Vatican established as separate state
Apr 15 Import tax on tea, imposed during reign of Elizabeth I, abolished
May 30 Labour Party returned to power under MacDonald
Aug 14 Singapore's floating dock officially opened
Oct 24 Wall Street crash heralded world economic crisis

1930 Jan 16 First patent of jet engine for aircraft taken out by Frank Whittle
Mar 2 D. H. Lawrence died, aged 42
Mar 6 Clarence Birdseye's frozen foods first went on sale in USA
Mar 17 Gandhi resumed civil disobedience campaign against British in India
Mar 18 Planet Pluto discovered
Apr 3 Haile Selassie became Emperor of Ethiopia
Apr 30 Telephone service between Britain and Australia inaugurated
May 5-29 Amy Johnson made solo flight from Britain to Australia in 20 days
Jun 16 Mixed bathing began in Serpentine, Hyde Park
Jun 29 Occupation of Germany by foreign troops came to an end after 11 years
Aug 21 Second daughter, Margaret Rose, born to Duchess of York
Oct 5 British airship R101 crashed in France on maiden voyage to India

1931 Feb 5 Malcolm Campbell set world land speed record of 246.575 mph in *Bluebird*
Mar 18 Jacob Schick's electric shaver produced
Apr 14 King Alphonso XIII of Spain exiled after republicans' victory in municipal elections
May 22 Whipsnade Zoo opened
Sept 21 Britain abandoned

Left, Al Jolson starred in the first talking picture, The Jazz Singer, *which opened in 1927.*

Above, Amy Johnson flew solo from Britain to Australia in May, 1930.

Gold Standard
Dec 9 Spain became a republic
Dec 11 Statute of Westminster introduced concept of "Commonwealth of Nations", confirming Dominions as autonomous and equal in status

1932
Jan 21 Lytton Strachey died, aged 51
Feb 4 Aldous Huxley's *Brave New World* published
Feb 10 Edgar Wallace died, aged 57
Feb 27 James Chadwick's discoveries of the neutron published in *Nature*
Mar 1 Britain abandoned free trade for first time since 1849
Mar 1 Lindbergh's baby son kidnapped and subsequently murdered
Mar 19 Sydney Harbour Bridge opened
May 9 Piccadilly Circus first lit by electricity
May 22 Amelia Earhart became first woman to fly solo across Atlantic in record time of 13½ hours
Jul 6 Kenneth Grahame died, aged 73
Jul 19 King and Queen opened Lambeth Bridge, linking Westminster and Lambeth
Sept 20 Saudi Arabia created under Ibn Saud
Oct 7 Beecham's London Philharmonic Orchestra made its debut

1933
Jan 30 Hitler became Chancellor of Germany
Jan 31 John Galsworthy died, aged 66
Feb 27 Nazis accused Communists of fire that destroyed Reichstag
Mar 4 Franklin Roosevelt inaugurated as 32nd US President
Apr 1 Persecution of Jews began in Germany
May 1 Telephone service between Britain and India inaugurated
Jul 14 Parties other than Nazis suppressed in Germany
Oct 14 Germany left international disarmament conference and withdrew from League of Nations
Nov 16 US established relations with USSR for first time since revolution
Dec 5 US prohibition repealed

1934
Feb 23 Sir Edward Elgar died, aged 76
Mar 26 Road Traffic Act introduced driving tests
May 28 Glyndebourne Festival Opera began its first season
Jun 8 Oswald Mosley addressed mass meeting of British Union of Fascists at Olympia
Jun 10 Frederick Delius died, aged 71
Jun 29-30 Purge of Nazi Party in "Night of the Long Knives" made Hitler undisputed leader of the Nazi Revolution. Sole executive power invested in him as Führer Aug 19

Left, the Duchess of York gave birth to a second daughter, Margaret Rose, on August 21, 1930.

Below, Sydney Harbour Bridge, Australia, which is 1,652 feet long, was opened on March 19, 1932.

Left, in November, 1934, the
Duke and Duchess of York
visited Mount Pleasant
sorting office in London.

Top, on February 27, 1933,
the Reichstag building in
Berlin was burnt down and,
on the pretext that it was a
Communist plot to seize power,
the Reich government
assumed emergency powers
thus beginning Hitler's
dictatorship.

Centre above, Adolf Hitler
took office as Chancellor of
Germany on January 30,
1933.

Above, Mao Tse-tung and the
major part of the Red Army
began what became known
as the Long March in October
1934 from Kiangsi 6,000 miles
across China to Shensi where
they arrived in October 1935.
Mao eventually established
the People's Republic of China
on October 1, 1949.

Right, Piccadilly, world
famous for its illuminated
advertisements, was first lit
by electricity on May 9, 1932.

13. Semaphores.
14. Searchlights.
15. Chart Room.
16. Wheel-House and Bridge.
17. Captain's and Officers' Quarters.
SUN DECK
18. Verandah Grill.
19. Engineer Officers' Accommodation.
20. Engineers' Ward Room.
21. Cinema Projection Room.
22. Gymnasium.
23. Squash Racquets Court.
24. Lift Gear.
25. Wireless Receiving Room.
26. Staterooms and Suites.
27. Forward Staircase and Lifts.
28. Staterooms and Suites.
PROMENADE DECK.
29. Cinema Projection Room.
30. Tourist Smoking Room.
31. Pantry.
32. Tourist Entrance.
33. Smoking Room.
41. Lounge.
42. Chair Stowage.
43. Writing Rooms.
44. Entrance.
45. Main Hall and Shopping Centre.
46. Drawing Room.
47. Altar.
48. Children's Playroom.
49. Forward Staircase and Lifts.
50. Cocktail Bar and Observation Lounge.
51. Promenade.
MAIN DECK.
52. Docking Bridge.
53. Tourist Lounge.
54. Tourist Staircase and Lifts.
55. Tourist Writing Room and Library.
56. Staterooms and Suites.
57. Staircase and Lifts.
58. Store Room.
59. Staterooms and Suites.
60. Main Staircase and Lifts.
61. Furniture Store.
62. Staterooms and Suites.
69. "A" Deck Tourist Lounge.
70. Tourist Entrance, Staircase and Lifts.
71. Suites and Bedroom Accommodation.
72. Staircase and Lifts.
73. Staterooms and Suites.
74. Staircase and Lifts.
75. Switch Room.
76, 77. Staterooms and Suites.
78. Staircase and Lifts.
79. Purser's Office.
80. Staterooms and Suites.
81. Forward Staircase and Lifts.
82. Third-Class Hairdresser's.
83. Third-Class Entrance.
84. Third-Class Smoking Room.
85. Fore Hatch.
86. Rope Store.
87. Forecastle and Anchor Capstan.
"B" DECK.
88. Crew.
89. Suites and Bedroom Accommodation.
98. Staircase and Lifts.
99. Hairdresser's and Beauty Parlour.
100. Staterooms and Suites.
101. Forward Staircase and Lifts.
102. Third-Class Children's Playroom.
103. Third-Class Lounge.
104. Mail-Handling Space.
105. Capstan Gear.
106. Crew.
"C" DECK.
107. Crew.
108. Capstan Space.
109. Bedroom Accommodation.
110. Staircase and Lifts.
111. Suites and Bedroom Accommodation.
112. Staircase and Lifts.
113. Tourist Dining Saloon.
114. Baker's Shop.
115. Vegetable-Preparing Room.
116. Kitchens.
117. Grill.
118. China Pantry.

Above, King George V and Queen Mary celebrated their Silver Jubilee in 1935. Frank Salisbury's painting of the reception at the west door of St Paul's Cathedral shows the Duke and Duchess of York, with the two princesses, just behind the Prince of Wales.

The liner Queen Mary *was launched on September 26, 1934.* The Illustrated London News *published this cut-away drawing on February 12 and called the Cunard liner "Britain's masterpiece of shipbuilding, which marks a new era in the efficiency and comfort of ocean travel."*

128. Crew.	156. Crew.	183. Shafts and Shaft Tunnels.
129. Suites and Bedroom Accommodation.	"E" DECK.	184. After Engine Rooms.
130. Baggage Lift Well.	158, 159, 160, 161. Suites and Bedroom Accommodation.	185. Forward Engine Rooms.
131. Suites and Bedroom Accommodation.	157. Crew.	186. Fan Rooms.
132. Tourist Staircase and Lifts.	162. Third-Class Accommodation.	187. No. 5 Boiler Room.
133. Suites and Bedroom Accommodation.	163. Mail Discharge Room.	188. Air-Condensing Plant.
134. Ales and Stout.	164. Special Room.	189. After Turbo-Generator Room.
135. Stores Entrance.	165. Crew.	190. Power Station.
136. Ice-Cream, Butter and Milk.		191. No. 4 Boiler Room.
137. Fruit-Ripening Room.	"F" DECK.	192. No. 3 Boiler Room.
138. Fruit Stores.	166. Tourist Baggage Room.	193. Forward Turbo-Generator Room.
139. Vegetable and Salad Room.	167. Bedroom Accommodation.	194. Power Station.
140. Fresh and Frozen Fish.	168. Tourist Swimming-Pool.	195. No. 2 Boiler Room.
141. Butcher's Shop and Meat Store.	169. Beer Stores.	196. No. 1 Boiler Room.
142. Poultry, Game, etc.	170. Lift Well.	197. Fan Rooms.
143. Bacon and Eggs.	171. Wines and Minerals.	198. Water-Softening Machinery.
144. Grocery Store.	172. Garage.	199. Tanks.
145. Hospital.	173. Registered Mail.	200. Baggage.
		201. Mail Space.
		202. General Cargo.
		203. Double Bottoms.

Jul 18 Mersey Tunnel opened
Sept 26 Cunard liner *Queen Mary* launched
Dec 8 Regular airmail service inaugurated between London and Australia

1935
Feb 1 Boulder (Hoover) Dam on Colorado River in Nevada and Arizona was completed, creating Lake Mead, largest reservoir in the world
Mar 16 Germany repudiated disarmament clauses of Versailles Treaty and reintroduced compulsory military service
Mar 21 Persia changed name to Iran
Apr 1 LCC's Green Belt scheme came into force
Apr 13 First regular air passenger service between Britain and Australia began
May 6 Silver Jubilee of George V's accession
Jul 30 First 10 Penguin books issued. Penguin No 1 was *Ariel*, a life of Shelley by André Maurois
Sept 15 Nuremberg Laws deprived Jews of German citizenship
Oct 3 Italian troops invaded Abyssinia without declaration of war
Oct 17 Ford's Model Y ("Popular") went on sale for £100

1936
Jan 18 Rudyard Kipling died, aged 70
Jan 20 George V died, aged 70. He was succeeded by his 41-year-old son as Edward VIII
Apr 30 A. E. Housman died, aged 77
May 5 Abyssinian War ended with Italian occupation of Addis Ababa
Jun 14 G. K. Chesterton died, aged 62
Jul 18 Right-wing army revolt started Spanish Civil War
Aug 1 Olympic Games opened in Berlin. Black American Jesse Owens won four gold medals
Aug 21 London University moved from Kensington to Bloomsbury
Aug 26 British military occupation of Egypt ended except for Canal Zone
Oct 1 London-Paris night ferry service inaugurated
Oct 5-9 Unemployed workers marched from Jarrow to London to seek government help
Nov 1 Hitler and Mussolini proclaimed Berlin-Rome "Axis"
Nov 2 BBC began regular TV transmissions from Alexandra Palace
Nov 25 Anti-Comintern Pact began German-Japanese cooperation
Nov 30 Crystal Palace destroyed by fire
Dec 10 Edward VIII abdicated in order to marry Mrs Simpson. He was succeeded by his brother as George VI
Dec 14 Order of the Garter conferred on Queen Elizabeth

Rudyard Kipling, author and poet, died on January 18, 1936.

Left, American Jesse Owens won four gold medals in the 1936 Berlin Olympic Games and set a world long jump record that stood for 25 years.

Below, Joseph Paxton's Crystal Palace, which had been removed to Sydenham after the Great Exhibition of 1851, was destroyed by fire on November 30, 1936.

Right, in 1936 unemployed workers marched from Jarrow in north-east England to London to present a petition to the government. Jarrow was one of the worst-hit areas in the depression of the 1930s.

On December 10, 1936, King Edward VIII abdicated in order to marry Mrs Wallis Simpson (they are pictured together, top, on holiday in Biarritz in 1934). Albert, Duke of York, succeeded to the throne as King George VI.

Queen Elizabeth
Sir Gerald Kelly, 1938

QUEEN ELIZABETH

With the best of intentions, but limited insight into the problems that lay ahead of the new King and his Queen Consort, Queen Mary told Lady Airlie that she was compiling "a little book on everything a Queen ought to know" for her daughter-in-law. Her friend said, "I saw her making notes for it in that clear, orderly handwriting."

It would have taken more even than a book of spells to deflect what Bertie had already sensed. "If the worst happens and I have to take over," he had written, "you can be assured that I shall do my best to clear up the inevitable mess . . . if the whole fabric does not crumble under the strain and shock of it all." He had decided to take his father's name and to be called King George VI in order to give a sense of continuity. When he became King on December 10, 1936, there had been two swift blows to the monarchy — a death and an abdication — within 10 months; and less than two years later his country would be at war, as some already feared.

In front of his wife he might be brave, but with his mother, the new King confessed, he "broke down and sobbed like a child" at the fate that had been thrust upon him.

His father had been slow to appreciate Bertie's qualities, but had recognised them clearly enough before he died. He declared that Bertie had "more guts than all his brothers put together". Now this courage, and all the new Queen's resources, were to be exercised and stretched as never before.

In private, both King and Queen had a keen sense of fun. Confirmation of his accession reached him while he was sitting at the luncheon table at 145 Piccadilly, and he asked his family, "Now, if someone comes through on the phone, who shall I say I am?" For the Queen, the joke was double-edged, for she realised that a potential problem lurked overseas in the form of the newly-named Duke of Windsor, the former Edward VIII.

And the telephone rang constantly with advice from the ex-King to the new King, often contrary to the judgments Bertie was receiving from his ministers. "This caused him trouble," said Walter Monckton, "which no one could understand who did not know the extent to which, before the abdication, the Duke of Windsor's brothers admired and looked up to him." Queen Elizabeth did. A stop was put to the calls. Even so, Mrs Belloc Lowndes found, some two years later, that "the King talks constantly of his brother . . . he seems haunted by him."

When the Duke of Windsor requested, shortly before the outbreak of war, that he should be allowed to return to Britain to play the part of a younger brother, Monckton, acting as intermediary, was probably right in divining another decision-maker behind the King: "I think the Queen felt plainly that it was undesirable to give the Duke any effective sphere of work. I felt then, as always, that she naturally thought that she must be on guard because the Duke of Windsor . . . might be the rallying-point for any who might be critical of the King, who was less superficially endowed with the arts and graces that please."

An Old Pretender.

Bertie had said he could face the future "with my wife and helpmeet by my side", and helpmeet was the perfect word to describe that blend of friend, partner, adviser and wife that made her his ideal Queen.

When he acceded, Bertie told his cousin, Lord Louis Mountbatten, that he was totally unprepared for the job: "I've never even seen a state paper. I'm only a naval officer." His father had never allowed him access to the despatch boxes. "There is no better training for a King," Mountbatten countered wisely.

Now the King took his consort into his confidence (as Victoria had done with Prince Albert), consulting her and telling Ministers, "I have spoken to the Queen and have decided . . ." Later he would describe the weight of kingship, which Edward VIII had described as "drudgery", as having been "almost too heavy but for the strength and comfort which I have always found in my home".

Elizabeth's multi-faceted new role of Queen, Consort, adviser, wife, mother of the new heir to the throne, daughter-in-law of a still formidable former Queen Consort and sister-in-law to a former King who perhaps would still be King, made Lady Airlie remark: "I pitied most of all the new Queen. In the 14 years of her marriage she had remained completely unspoiled, still at heart the simple unaffected girl I had known at Glamis, carrying out her public duties with an efficiency that won Queen Mary's admiration, but finding her true happiness in her home and her own family circle."

One of the first shocks was the move to Buckingham Palace on February 15, 1937, at which Lilibet lamented, "We shall have to live behind railings." The Palace was hardly cosy: more like a monument to the past, "a sepulchure", in the Duke of Windsor's words. But, soon noticing feminine touches typical of the Queen, a friend exclaimed, "It looks home-like already." The King smiled proudly, and declared, "Elizabeth could make a home anywhere."

A greater shock, though it had been expected for some time because she had been ill, was the death of the Queen's mother, Lady Strathmore, just as the King and Queen were to visit Paris. Rather than cancel the visit the Queen decided it should be postponed for three weeks while her clothes for the trip were copied entirely in white — used before as a Royal colour for mourning. The visit was triumphant. Lady Diana Cooper commented, "Each night's flourish outdid the last."

With greater insight into both personal and international relations Violet Trefusis described a particularly ornate evening at the Quai d'Orsay when the couple outwitted formality. "The King and Queen consulted no one; they exchanged a look of mischievous complicity, took hands and raced through the room like a couple of children. When they were seen hand in hand, and unaccompanied on the balcony, the people of Paris went mad." One newspaper commented, "France has a monarchy again." After the war, de Gaulle told them, "You are the only two people who have always shown me humanity and understanding."

Still more important in political terms was their visit to Canada and the United States in May and June, 1939. "When I induced their Majesties to visit me out here, I didn't realise I was pulling the string of such a shower-bath," wrote the Governor General, Lord Tweedsmuir. "The Queen has a perfect genius for the right kind of publicity. The unrehearsed episodes were marvellous."

Unrehearsed they may have been, but not unpremeditated. The Queen later described to Mrs Eleanor Roosevelt her technique of picking out individuals at different levels of the crowd and really looking at them, so that a whole group would be infected by one person's delighted exclamation, "She looked at me." And showing that she was as quick on her toes here as on the dance floor, she replied, when asked whether she was Scottish or English, "Since we've reached Quebec I've been a Canadian." She then went on to spend 10 minutes chatting to some Scottish stonemasons who were thrilled by talk of home. In the intense heat of Washington the Queen felt faint; after that some people noticed that the Royal couple seemed to try to halve the work for each other by talking to alternate people.

The Queen's childhood penchant for dressing up now acquired a new relevance. A flowing gown was designed to enchant those who gathered to see her at halts breaking the train's long chuntering through the nights, and when a little girl was disappointed by her daytime outfit she insisted that the child should be brought to see her in evening dress. The child was more transformed than the Queen: "Oh Daddy!" she cried, "I have seen the Fairy Queen."

When the tour had finished, the Queen declared, "It made us, the King and I." Ironically, though it had begun this process, it was the war that was to complete it, exacting at the same time its own price for their success.

State visits had always meant family separations. But the outbreak of the Second World War, on September 3, 1939 (only six weeks after Princess Elizabeth had met a fairhaired naval cadet, Philip Mountbatten, at Dartmouth) inflicted subtler wounds on family life.

The two princesses were considered safest at Windsor. They were being educated privately so no upheaval in their schooling was involved. Queen Mary spent the duration at Badminton in the West Country.

The King and Queen continued to spend their days in London at Buckingham Palace, returning to the family group and comparative peace of Windsor for dinner — though not every night. But every morning, if they were at Windsor, they left at 8am for the drive to London where they would often lunch alone with Winston Churchill and, remembering that

"Careless talk costs lives", serve themselves. One young guardsman, quoted by Elizabeth Longford, remembered, "One evening [the Queen] returned late from London after a *dreadful* day. Hundreds of houses down, streets up, people crying. The lot. But she came down to the Quadrangle to see us at the household dinner in the Star Chamber, as she always did, and laughed and joked with the children. And *what* she was like with the King, forever loving and soothing."

Such was her spirit that her biographer, David Duff, said she was "Britain's secret weapon in World War II", while Hitler admitted she was "the most dangerous woman in Europe".

In 1940 it was suggested that Canada might provide a refuge for the princesses, but the Queen said, "They could not go without me, I could not go without the King, and the King will never go." She now felt so rooted at Windsor that she declared, "I should die if I had to leave."

Old skills came in handy. She practised shooting in the grounds of the Palace — "They won't take me easily" — broadcast to the women of France in their own language, and thanked those she had met or seen in the US, and their compatriots, for their "compassion . . . which has been for 2,000 years the mark of the good neighbour". She knew, too, when not to appear too well off. When President and Mrs Roosevelt visited Britain in 1942, the latter reported finding a spartan regime with a one-bar electric fire in each room except the small drawing room — allowed coal — and "except for game . . . nothing . . . that was not served in any ordinary war canteen".

The real danger for the Royal Family, as for the rest of Britain, was not starvation — surveys showed less malnutrition because a balanced diet was enforced on people — but

bombing. Buckingham Palace was bombed nine times. On one occasion, the King recorded, they watched bombs falling into the quadrangle and "were out into the passage as fast as we could get there . . . We all wondered why we weren't dead." On another occasion the Queen waited for him while he went upstairs to retrieve a corgi (already her favourite breed of dog) before they fled to the shelter.

"I am glad we have been bombed," decided the Queen. "I feel I can look the East End in the face." And that she did, literally, visiting bombed sites, drinking tea with people during an alert, and always noticing the individual difficulty. Once a dog refused to leave the debris of his former home and she said, "Perhaps I can help. I am rather good with dogs." She proved it by kneeling down and coaxing him out.

The Queen saw far more of the war than most civilians. She indefatigably visited bombed cities, factories, hospitals, dockyards, always looking her best — in deliberately chosen "dusty" colours that would not soil too quickly. Everywhere they were seen the Royal couple's attitude boosted morale: "I anticipated her charm," noted Harold Nicolson. "What astonished me is how the King is changed. He is now like his brother. He is so gay and she so calm. They did me all the good in the world. We shall win."

When the King insisted on flying to El Alamein in June, 1943, she, left behind, "imagined every sort of horror and walked up and down my room staring at the telephone". Before he left the King had created her a Counsellor of State so that she could preside over ceremonies in the event of his absence — a daunting honour.

In 1942 the King's youngest brother, the Duke of Kent, was killed in action and in 1944 many of the King and Queen's friends were among the

121 dead when the Guards Chapel near Buckingham Palace was bombed. It was, said Miss Crawford, "the one and only time during the whole war when I saw the Queen really shaken." Then, in November that year, her father died.

Yet there were happy events too in 1944. Princess Elizabeth celebrated her 18th birthday and was herself created a Counsellor of State. Soon afterwards, in June, 1944, came D-Day and, the next year, in March 1945, the Princess was allowed to join the Auxiliary Territorial Service, driving and servicing heavy lorries, and, her mother laughed, "We had sparking plugs during the whole of dinner last night."

Outwardly cheerful, the Queen wrote to Queen Mary, "I feel quite exhausted after seeing and hearing so much sadness, sorrow, heroism and magnificent spirit. The destruction is so awful, the people so *wonderful* — they deserve a better world."

On May 7, 1945, came the news of victory in Europe and Hitler's suicide. From Windsor the King spoke, for them both, with characteristic modesty, "We have only tried to do our duty during these five-and-a-half years."

"Poor darlings," wrote the King in his diary on VE day, thinking of his daughters. "They have never had any fun yet."

Like any happy husband and wife, the King and Queen were looking forward to some peace and pleasure together, little dreaming that less than seven years of married life were left to them. Both were suffering from fatigue. The King said he felt "burned out" and, as a visitor noticed, was "inclined to be rather excitable". In the family his tendency to fly into a tantrum, known at home as a "gnash", was well known. The Queen dealt with it by suffering an attack of vagueness, another trick she had learnt from her mother; Princess Margaret practised such diversions as throwing a spoon over her shoulder to make everyone laugh, a variation on *her* mother's capacity for changing the subject, or imitating someone in an accurate and irresistibly funny way.

The sisters were now 19 and nearly 15, and the contrast between their characters and personalities, evident even as toddlers, was accentuated. As heir to the throne Princess Elizabeth had received a more profound education than her sister: no one seems to have taken seriously the possibility of the younger sister succeeding. Lilibet was grave and reserved and, according to Lady Airlie, "One of the most unselfish girls I have ever met, always the first to give way in any of the small issues that arise in every home." She was in many ways her father's daughter. She had inherited his modesty, his agonising conscientiousness, and could be as easily put out. She had made up her mind, in the same way as he had, who she wanted to marry, and would do so.

In her younger daughter the Queen found the fun-loving, available and pretty daughter every mother longs to spoil with pretty clothes, parties and fancy-free enjoyment, recapturing the carefree idea of youth. The King, noticed Lady Airlie, "spoiled Princess Margaret, and continued to treat her as an *enfant terrible*". Neither parent foresaw nor prepared her for deep personal wounds in life. She was brought up, as her mother had been, to think of herself as a future wife and mother trained for no role outside the "family firm" and had not been encouraged to have serious outside interests. But, unlike her sister, who had now known Philip Mountbatten for six years and whose future role as Queen looked sure, she had not settled her affections on anyone.

The King had the strain of a new government to cope with and, early in 1946, he wrote, "My new government is not too easy and the people are rather difficult to talk to . . . still learning how to run their departments." Prime Minister Attlee, for his part, found the King "rather a worrying type," but noted, "In all his work he had the help and support of the gracious lady who was an ideal Consort."

After the first post-war Christmas at Sandringham a visitor wrote: "I thought — regretfully at first — how much the atmosphere had changed . . . The radio, worked by Princess Elizabeth, blared incessantly. Before the end of the week I revised my impressions. There was no denying that the new atmosphere at Sandringham was very much more friendly than in the old days, more like that of any home. One senses far more the setting of ordinary family life . . . It was the way in which the King said 'You must ask Mummy' when his daughters wanted to do something — just as any father would do."

As early as January 1941, the Conservative MP Henry ("Chips") Channon had said of Philip Mountbatten, "Extraordinarily handsome . . . he is to be our Prince Consort." Princess Elizabeth's happiness in his company spoke for itself. But for once the King put his foot down saying, "We both think she is too young for that now . . . She has never met any young men of her own age . . . I like Philip. He is intelligent, has a sense of humour and thinks of things in the right way . . . P had better not think any more about it at present."

In 1947 there was a wonderful family holiday to look forward to — a three-month visit to South Africa, which would also serve as a testing time for the feelings of Lilibet and Philip. Group Captain Peter Townsend, an equerry to the King, was included in the party.

Princess Elizabeth admitted, "While we were scorching, we felt rather guilty at being away from it all." Post-war Britain was deep in the doldrums now that the enemy was no longer Germany but a general drabness and shortages.

The Queen, however, luxuriating in moments of relaxation on board HMS *Vanguard* before the very strenuous work of the tour proper began, showed her powers of expression and capacity for enjoyment in one brief phrase. As they entered warmer climes she commented, "It's like being stroked." But whatever the delights of scenery, sun, exotic foods and admiration, nothing blunted her Scottish mind. When a Boer veteran said bluntly, "We sometimes feel we cannot forgive the English," she soothingly responded, "I understand perfectly. We feel very much the same in Scotland too."

"She was indefatigable," said Peter Townsend afterwards. "The King owed so much to the gracious — and tenacious — support of the Queen." Nor did she lack physical courage. When a Zulu ran towards their car she made what she later called "the worst mistake of my life", beating him off with her parasol till it broke; he was then beaten senseless by policemen. In his hand was a 10 shilling note he had wanted to give to Princess Elizabeth.

Determined always to look her best in public, the Queen set out in unsuitable shoes to visit the tomb of Cecil Rhodes and had to borrow Lilibet's sandals. Her daughter, who had to walk in stockings, commented, "It was so like Mummy to set out in those shoes."

They returned to London on May 12 — the 10th anniversary of the Coronation, yet aeons away in experience and confidence.

Only three months later, on August 15, 1947, India became independent. The King was no longer an Emperor; but he was a King proud of his country, his family and himself and recognised that he was "the most fortunate of men".

On November 20, 1947, Princess Elizabeth married Prince Philip, now Duke of Edinburgh. She evidently described her happiness to her mother, for the King wrote to her, "I was so glad you wrote and told Mummy . . . I was rather afraid that you had thought I was being hard-hearted about it . . . Our family, us four, the 'Royal Family', must remain together with additions of course at suitable moments! I have watched you grow up all these years with pride under the skilful direction of Mummy, who as you know is the most marvellous person in the world in my eyes . . ."

Intense joy and grief now lay ahead of the Queen. "Looking back over 25 years," she said on the Silver Jubilee of her wedding in April, 1948, "and to my own happy childhood, I realise more and more the wonderful sense of security and happiness which comes from a loving home." A few months later, in November, her first grandchild, Prince Charles, was born. He was to bring her immense joy and companionship.

By now she knew that the King was suffering from arteriosclerosis. Gangrene was a danger and the amputation of a leg was discussed, but an operation obviated this.

The King and Queen's second grandchild, Princess Anne, was born in August, 1950, an oasis of further joy amid much worry. Only 13 months later the King was told he must have his left lung removed. The Queen insisted on being told the truth: he had cancer. Deciding he must never know this she embarked on the greatest performance of her life.

Acting again as a Counsellor of State she attended to public matters; at home she continued to make life as smooth, happy and comfortable as possible for the King, determined to show gaiety and enthusiasm to the last.

On December 11, 1951, the King and Queen celebrated the 15th anniversary of their accession and, three days later, the King's 56th birthday. It was to be his last. On January 30 the whole family went to see the American musical *South Pacific* before Princess Elizabeth and the Duke of Edinburgh set off on the first part of a tour that was intended to take them to Australia, but which ended in Kenya. As the King waved goodbye to them at London Airport, Oliver Lyttelton, the Colonial Secretary, "was shocked by the King's appearance . . . I felt with deep foreboding that this was to be the last time he would see his daughter, and that he thought so himself."

Less than a week of life was left to the King; less than a week as Queen to his consort. On February 5 he had a good day's shooting at Sandringham, the total bag being 480 hares and two rabbits, while the Queen and Princess Margaret were visiting a friend, the artist Edward Seago, in another part of Norfolk.

"I got back to Sandringham rather late, and, as I always did, rushed straight to the King's room," wrote the Queen when she thanked Seago for the day with him and the pictures he had sent back with them. "He [the King] was enchanted with them all, and we spent a very happy time looking at them together. We had a truly gay dinner with the King, like his old self . . ." That night, his bedroom door open so that he would be heard if he called out, the King died in his sleep.

Chapter 4, Queen Elizabeth The Queen Mother, follows on page 60.

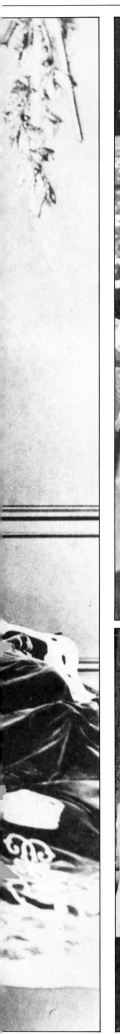

King George VI was crowned on May 12, 1937. Far left, the Royal family at Buckingham Palace after the ceremony.

Left, the Archbishop of Canterbury, Dr Cosmo Lang, placed the crown on Queen Elizabeth's head.

Above, Princess Elizabeth arriving at Westminster Abbey.

Below, the King and Queen together with Queen Mary, and their daughters acknowledged the crowds from the Buckingham Palace balcony.

1937

Jan 23 Stalin began purges of Communist Party
Feb 15 King George and Queen Elizabeth moved to Buckingham Palace
Feb 16 American Wallace Carothers patented Nylon
Apr 27 Basque town of Guernica annihilated by bombing in Spanish Civil War
May 6 German airship *Hindenburg* exploded at Lakehurst, New Jersey
May 12 King George VI's coronation
May 27 Golden Gate Bridge, San Francisco, opened
Jun 19 J. M. Barrie died, aged 77
Jul 2 Amelia Earhart disappeared on flight over Pacific
Jul 7 Japanese forces invaded China. Undeclared war continued until 1945
Jul 23 Divorce proceedings facilitated in England and Wales by Matrimonial Causes Bill
Oct 28 Spanish Government moved to Barcelona
Dec 11 Italy withdrew from League of Nations
Dec 29 Irish Free State adopted name of Eire
Royal tours: King George and Queen Elizabeth paid official visit to Belfast

1938

Jan 4 Britain postponed scheme for partition of Palestine
Feb 4 Hitler assumed office of war minister
Mar 6 Trolley buses started to replace trams in London
Mar 12 Austria occupied by German army and *Anschluss* with Germany proclaimed next day
Aug 20 Len Hutton scored 364 runs in Oval Test against Australia
Sept 27 Queen Elizabeth launched Cunard liner which bore her name
Sept 29 Following talks with Hitler at Munich Prime Minister Chamberlain accepted Germany's occupation of Sudetenland in Czechoslovakia to secure "peace in our time"
Nov 9 Deportation of Jews to concentration camps began
Dec 18 First nuclear fission of uranium produced by physicist Otto Hahn
Royal tours: King George and Queen Elizabeth visited Paris

1939

Mar 28 Spanish War ended with victory for General Franco
Mar 31 Britain and France pledged support to Poland when Hitler denounced 1934 non-aggression pact
Apr 7 Italian troops invaded Albania
May 22 Hitler and Mussolini signed 10-year political and military alliance
May 24 Plan for independent Palestine by 1949 approved by British Parliament, later denounced by both Jews and

Above, Pablo Picasso's painting Guernica *was inspired by the artist's anger at the bombing of the Basque town of Guernica by pro-Franco forces in 1937 during the Spanish Civil War.*

Above, the Queen visited a mothercraft centre at Highgate on June 22, 1938. Earlier that month she had visited a Girl Guide rally, left, with her daughters.

Above left, 35 people died when the hydrogen-filled German airship Hindenburg *exploded and burnt as it was approaching the mooring mast at Lakehurst, New Jersey.*

Right, The Illustrated London News *of June 4, 1938, printed this illustration by H. Rutherford, a "television artist", of "Television at Alexandra Palace". Public test transmissions were first made from Alexandra Palace in October, 1936.*

Arabs

Aug 23 USSR signed non-aggression pact with Germany

Aug 27 Heinkel He 178 made first jet-propelled flight in Germany

Sept 1 Germany invaded Poland

Sept 2 National Service Act called up men aged 20-41

Sept 3 Britain and France declared war on Germany

Sept 4 Winston Churchill appointed First Lord of Admiralty

Sept 17 Poland invaded by USSR from east. West Poland incorporated into German Reich Oct 8

Sept 30 British expeditionary forces landed in France

Nov 30 USSR invaded Finland

Dec 17 German battleship *Graf Spee* scuttled in Montevideo

Dec 14 USSR expelled from League of Nations

Royal tours: King George and Queen Elizabeth visited North America

1940

Jan 8 Food rationing began in Britain

Feb 21 Women received pensions at 60

Apr 1 State owned BOAC assumed responsibility for both Imperial and British Airways

Apr 9 German forces invaded Norway and Denmark

May 10 German forces overran Belgium, Netherlands and Luxembourg

Churchill became Prime Minister of coalition government

Local Defence Volunteers (later Home Guard) formed

May 15 First Nylon stockings went on sale in USA

May 27-Jun 3 Trapped British army evacuated from Dunkirk

Jun 10 Italy entered war as German ally

Jun 14 German forces occupied Paris. Armistice signed Jun 22

Jul 3 French fleet sunk by British warships at Oran, North Africa

Jul 10 German aircraft attacked southern England in large numbers to begin Battle of Britain

Jul 23 Purchase tax imposed

Aug 20 Trotsky assassinated in Mexico

Sept 7 All-night bombing raid began the Blitz

Sept 12 Lascaux caves discovered

Sept 13 Buckingham Palace bombed

Sept 24 George VI instituted George Cross for civilian gallantry

Sept 27 Germany, Italy and Japan united in 10-year military and economic alliance

Nov 11 Italian fleet crippled by British attack at Taranto

1941

Apr 11 Blitz on Coventry

Apr 16 Britain received first US Lend-lease shipments of food

Top, the first flight of a turbojet-powered aircraft was made in Germany by a Heinkel HE178 on August 27, 1939.

Above, the King and Queen, with their daughters, join in the singing at the King's Scout Camp, Abergeldie, near Balmoral in August, 1939.

Left, the King and Queen acknowledging cheers in Montreal during their 1939 North American tour.

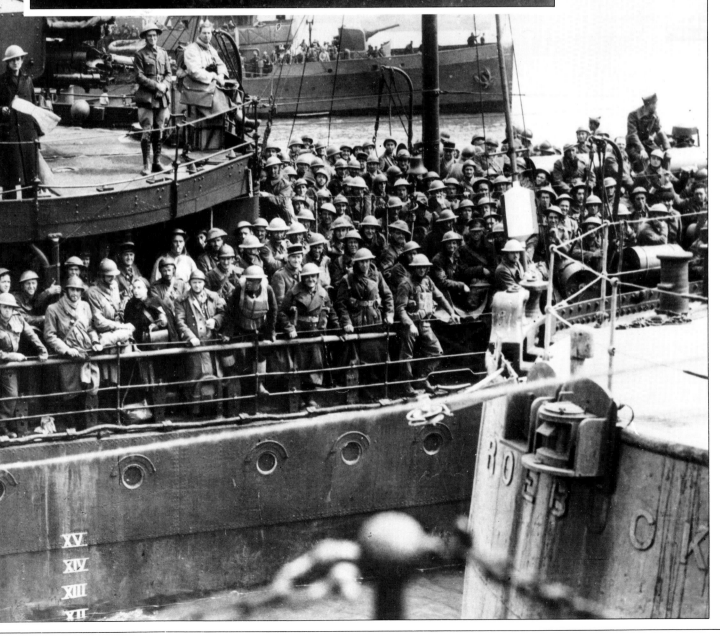

Left, Germany invaded Poland on September 1, 1939.

Below, in May, 1940, the British expeditionary force and other Allied troops, isolated by the Germans, were evacuated from Dunkirk to England on naval vessels and on hundreds of civilian boats.

May 5 Ethiopia liberated by British troops, Haile Selassie reinstalled as Emperor

May 4 Double summer time introduced

May 10 Rudolf Hess flew to Scotland on abortive peace mission

Jun 8 Britain and France invaded Syria to prevent establishment of Axis bases

Jun 22 USSR invaded by German troops

Jul 12 Anglo-Russian agreement of mutual assistance signed in Morocco

Aug 14 Atlantic Charter, eight-point declaration of war aims, issued by Churchill and Roosevelt

Dec 7 US naval base at Pearl Harbour, Hawaii, attacked by Japanese aircraft

Dec 8 US and Britain declared war on Japan

Dec 11 US declared war on Germany and Italy

Dec 25 Hong Kong fell to Japan

1942

Feb 1 British forces in Malaya withdrew to Singapore, which surrendered to Japan Feb 15

Apr 16 Malta awarded George Cross for valour in resisting German air attacks

May 30 Cologne bombed by RAF in first mass air attack on German industrial targets

May 31 Gestapo chief Reinhard Heydrich assassinated by Czech patriots

Jun 4 Japan's expansion in central Pacific ended by Battle of Midway

Jun 22 Walter Sickert died, aged 82

Aug 19 Heavy casualties sustained in Dieppe raid by British and Canadian troops

Aug 25 Duke of Kent killed on active service, aged 39

Oct 23 Battle of El Alamein began campaign to clear North Africa of Axis troops

Dec 1 William Beveridge's *A Report on Social Insurance and Allied Services* published

Dec 2 Chain reaction in uranium demonstrated by Enrico Fermi

1943

Jan 31 German army surrendered at Stalingrad. 90,000 prisoners taken

Feb 13 Nuffield Foundation for medical, scientific and social research created

May 12 Axis troops in North Africa surrendered

May 16 Jewish rebellion in Warsaw ghetto crushed

Jun 4 Free French leader Charles de Gaulle formed French Committee of National Liberation

Jun 12-25 King George visited North Africa. Queen Elizabeth made Counsellor of State in his absence

Jul 10 Anglo-American troops landed in Sicily

Sept 3 Italy surrendered and joined war against Germany

Oct 13

Below, the King's younger brother, the Duke of Kent, was killed in action on August 25, 1942.

Below centre, the King and Queen visited Southern Command, where they inspected tanks and watched a mock battle.

Below, an official portrait of the King and Queen taken at Buckingham Palace during the Second World War.

Bottom, the King and Queen frequently visited bombed areas of London to inspect the damage and talk to residents.

Much of the city of London was destroyed by bombs and fire during the Second World War but St Paul's Cathedral escaped with relatively minor damage.

Top, Warsaw's Jews were confined to a ghetto by the Nazi administration in Poland. After nearly 400,000 had been removed to concentration camps some 60,000 survivors rebelled. The uprising was crushed on May 16, 1943.

Above, the second battle of El Alamein, the turning point of the struggle in Africa, began on October 23, 1942.

Nov 28-Dec 1 Allied summit meeting in Teheran attended by Roosevelt, Churchill and Stalin

Nov 29 Marshal Tito established government in Yugoslavia

1944
Jan 1 Sir Edwin Lutyens died, aged 75

Feb 28 British forces began reconquest of Burma

Apr 6 PAYE income tax introduced

Jun 4 Allied troops captured Rome from German forces

Jun 6 Allied invasion of Europe began with landings on Normandy coast

Jun 13 First V1 "doodlebug" hit London

Jul 20 Assassination attempt on Hitler failed

Aug 3 Education Act introduced free secondary education for all

Aug 19 Henry Wood died, aged 75

Aug 25 Paris liberated. De Gaulle set up provisional French government

Sept 4 Allies captured Antwerp and two days later, Brussels

Sept 8 First V2 rocket fell on Britain

Sept 26 British airborne forces failed to capture bridge at Arnhem

Dec 16 German forces under von Rundstedt mounted Battle of the Bulge offensive in Ardennes

1945
Jan 9 US forces invaded Philippines under command of General MacArthur

Jan 17 Soviet forces captured Warsaw

Mar 13 Allied forces commanded West Bank of Rhine

Mar 25 David Lloyd George died, aged 81

Mar 28 Last of 1,052 V2 rockets fell on Britain

Apr 12 President Roosevelt died, aged 63. He was succeeded by Harry S. Truman

Apr 21 Soviet troops entered Berlin, which surrendered May 2

Apr 28 Mussolini executed by Italian partisans

Apr 30 Hitler committed suicide

May 3 Allies entered Hamburg

May 7 Germany surrendered unconditionally at Rheims

Jul 17 First atom bomb exploded in New Mexico desert

Jul 26 General election won by Labour Party with Clement Attlee as Prime Minister

Aug 6 US dropped atom bomb on Hiroshima

Aug 9 Atom bomb dropped on Nagasaki

Aug 14 Japan surrendered

Sept 2 Ho Chi Minh proclaimed Vietnam independent

Oct 24 United Nations created

Nov 20 Nuremberg trial of Nazi War criminals began

Dec 27 International Monetary Fund established

Top, the Allied invasion of Europe began with landings on the Normandy coast on June 6, 1944. This drawing, which appeared in the June 17 issue of the Sphere, *shows tanks and troops leaving the landing craft.*

Above, Paris was liberated on August 25, 1944.

Right, crowds gathered at Piccadilly Circus in London on VE Day, May 8, 1945, after Germany's unconditional surrender ended the war in Europe.

Inset, atomic bombs were dropped on Hiroshima and Nagasaki early in August and Japan surrendered on August 14. On August 15, VJ Day, inset right, the Royal family acknowledged the cheers of the crowd from the balcony of Buckingham Palace.

1946

Jan 3 William Joyce ("Lord Haw Haw") executed for treason

Jan 10 UN General Assembly met in London. Resumed in New York Oct 23

Feb 24 Juan Peron became President of Argentina

Mar 5 Churchill appealed to West to stand up to Russia in speech at Fulton Missouri, in which he coined phrase "Iron Curtain"

Feb 14 Government took over Bank of England

May 21 Heathrow Airport formally opened

Jun 7 BBC resumed regular TV programmes

Jul 21 World wheat shortage led to bread rationing (until July 1948)

Jul 29-Oct 15 Peace conference of 21 nations met in Paris

Sept 29 BBC's Third Programme inaugurated to supplement "Home Service" and "Light Programme"

Nov 3 Power in Japan transferred from Emperor to elected assembly

Dec 11 First stored-programme computer patented

1947

Jan 1 Coal industry nationalized

Feb 20 Lord Mountbatten appointed last Viceroy of India

Mar 12 President Truman outlined doctrine of economic and military aid to states threatened by communism

Apr 1 Compulsory school leaving age raised to 15

Apr 21 Princess Elizabeth broadcast to people of British Commonwealth and Empire from South Africa on her coming of age

Apr 30 Land Rover introduced

Jun 5 Marshall Plan set out US aid programme for European recovery

Jul 8 Edwin Land invented the Polaroid camera

Aug 15 India and Pakistan become independent Dominions

Aug 24 Edinburgh Festival of Arts began first season

Oct 13 Sidney Webb (Lord Passfield) died aged 88

Oct 14 First supersonic flight by Bell XS-1 American aircraft

Nov 20 Princess Elizabeth married Philip Mountbatten, Duke of Edinburgh, in Westminster Abbey

Nov 29 UN approved partition of Palestine in spite of rejection by Arabs and Jews

Dec 14 Stanley, Earl Baldwin, died aged 80

Royal tours: King George and Queen Elizabeth, with two Princesses, visited South Africa

1948

Jan 1 British railways nationalized

Jan 4 Burma became independent

Jan 20 Gandhi assassinated

Feb 4 Ceylon became independent

Top, Princess Elizabeth married Philip Mountbatten, Duke of Edinburgh, on November 20, 1947.

Above, Lord Louis Mountbatten was appointed Viceroy of India on February 20, 1947. As the last Viceroy he administered the transfer of power to India and Pakistan on August 15 that year.

Right, the Land Rover, first manufactured in April, 1947.

Far right, King George VI and Queen Elizabeth celebrated their Silver Wedding on April 26, 1948.

Mar 20 USSR left Allied Control Commission and began blockade of West Berlin

Apr 1 Electricity production nationalized

Apr 26 King George and Queen Elizabeth celebrated Silver Wedding

May 14 State of Israel founded. Arab neighbours refused to recognize it and invaded on May 15

Jun 5 Aldeburgh Festival of Music founded by Benjamin Britten

Jun 21 LP record invented by Peter Goldmark

Jun 24 Western powers began airlift to overcome blockade of West Berlin

Jul 5 National Health Service inaugurated

Jul 15 Transistor invented by John Bardeen and Walter Brattain

Jul 16 First flight of Vickers Viscount turboprop airliner

Jul 29 Olympic Games opened at Wembley Stadium

Aug 15 Formal division of Korea established with foundation of Republic of Korea in the South

Sept 9 Korean People's Democratic Republic founded in North

Nov 14 Prince Charles born to Princess Elizabeth

Nov 23 Royal visit to Australia cancelled due to King's illness

Dec 12 National Service conscription for men aged 18-26 introduced

1949 Feb 1 Clothes rationing ended

Mar 31 Newfoundland became Canadian province

Apr 4 North Atlantic Treaty signed by Belgium, Britain, Canada, Denmark, France, Iceland, Italy, Luxembourg, Netherlands, Norway, Portugal and US

Apr 20 HMS *Amethyst* fired on and detained by communists on Yangtse-Kiang during Chinese revolution. Escaped Jul 30

Apr 12 Eire, proclaimed republic, left Commonwealth

May 5 Council of Europe established in Strasbourg

May 12 USSR ended blockade of Berlin

May 23 German Federal Republic (West Germany) established

May 26 South Africa adopted apartheid as official policy

Jul 16 Chinese nationalist forces withdrew to Formosa under President Chiang Kaishek

Jul 27 First flight of De Havilland Comet jet airliner

Sept 18 Pound devalued from $4.03 to $2.80

Sept 20 Berlin airlift ended after 277,264 flights

Oct 1 People's Republic of China proclaimed under Mao Tse-tung

Oct 7 German Democratic Republic (East Germany) established

Nov 24 UK iron and steel in-

dustries nationalized

1950

Jan 21 George Orwell died, aged 47
Jan 31 US Atomic Energy Commission began development of hydrogen bomb
Feb 14 USSR and China signed 30-year alliance treaty
Mar 8 USSR announced it had atom bomb
Jun 25 Communist North Korean forces invaded South Korea
Aug 15 Princess Anne born to Princess Elizabeth
Sept 11 Jan Smuts died, aged 80
Sept 26 Nato decided to form integrated European defence force
Oct 2 Legal aid came into operation in Britain
Nov 2 George Bernard Shaw died, aged 94
Dec 13 "X" certificate introduced by British film censors
Dec 25 Stone of Scone stolen by Scottish nationalists from Westminster Abbey

1951

Jan 1 First episode of *The Archers* broadcast by BBC
Apr 14 Ernest Bevin died, aged 70
May 3 Festival of Britain opened
May 25 British diplomats Guy Burgess and Donald Maclean defected to USSR
Sept 23 George VI underwent operation for lung resection at Buckingham Palace
Oct 6 British High Commissioner in Malaya, Henry Gurney, assassinated
Oct 25 Conservative Government elected. Winston Churchill became Prime Minister for second time

1952

Feb 6 George VI died of lung cancer, aged 56, after a reign of 15 years. His 25-year-old daughter flew home from visit to East Africa to ascend the throne as Elizabeth II
Feb 18 Greece and Turkey joined Nato
Apr 28 Eisenhower resigned post of Supreme Allied Commander to fight US presidential elections
Apr 28 Occupying forces withdrawn from Japan
May 7 Geoffrey Dummer published concept of the integrated circuit
Jul 6 Last tram ran in London
Jul 23 General Neguib seized power in Egypt. King Farouk was forced to abdicate
Aug 11 Hussein proclaimed King of Jordan
Oct 3 Britain tested atomic bomb in Monte Bello Islands, NW Australia
Oct 20 State of emergency declared in Kenya following Mau Mau violence against white settlers
Nov 1 First hydrogen bomb exploded by US in Pacific
Nov 25 Agatha Christie's *The Mousetrap* began West End run of more than 30 years

Above, Harry Oakes played Dan Archer in the first episode of The Archers, *which was broadcast on January 1, 1951.*

Left, Princess Anne was born on August 15, 1950. She is pictured here at her christening in October held by her mother, Princess Elizabeth. With her are Queen Mary, King George VI and Queen Elizabeth, the Duke of Edinburgh and Prince Charles

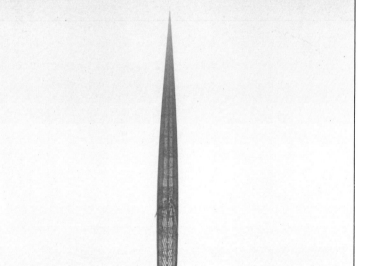

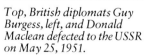

Top, British diplomats Guy Burgess, left, and Donald Maclean defected to the USSR on May 25, 1951.

Above, the last tram ran in London on July 6, 1952.

The Festival of Britain was opened by the King on May 3, 1951. The Skylon, left, was illuminated internally by a series of lamps grouped in clusters of three around a central steel tube. Burnished aluminium cones reflected the light on to external reflectors.

Top left, the King and Queen had paid a visit to the Festival of Britain site on the south bank of the Thames in London to see the work in progress.

Above, Agatha Christie's The Mousetrap opened at the Ambassadors Theatre in London in 1952, with Richard Attenborough and Sheila Sim in the original cast.

Left, the King, Queen and Princess Margaret were at the airport when Princess Elizabeth and the Duke of Edinburgh left for their tour of Australasia in January, 1952. The King died on February 6 and his elder daughter returned to England as Queen Elizabeth II.

Queen Elizabeth the Queen Mother
Michael Noakes, 1978-79

CHAPTER 4

QUEEN ELIZABETH THE QUEEN MOTHER

Swans, the birds of royalty, mate for life. So it was for King George VI and Queen Elizabeth. Now with the King's death when she was only 51 many years of isolation must have seemed to loom ahead of his widow. A Queen Consort's place in the Constitution is defined by law and by custom; once widowed she has no such fixed status. Her first thought was of the succession and her daughter. "We must tell Elizabeth: we must tell the Queen," she said; and so Prince Philip broke the news to his wife in Kenya and they returned for the state funeral. Even after this she remained in a state of unreality well-known to many who have been bereaved. "One cannot yet believe that it has all happened, one feels rather dazed," she wrote to Edward Seago.

Others now began fully to realise how right her marriage to the King had been in its interdependence — each had given much, and each had rewarded the other's generosity by taking much. Her sister Rose, Lady Granville, had noted long before, "The King was a rock to her. In all fundamental things the Queen was sustained by the King." Her other sister Mary, Lady Elphinstone, had realised that they were "particularly together. Both leaned so much on each other."

Now those who had seen her as the sustainer of the two saw a new vulnerability in her, overnight. "She had great difficulties when the King died. She had lost her companion and the job at once. It took her a long time to realise how much she was still needed," said a friend who later, when she herself was in a similar situation, found her "utterly understanding, without being sentimental".

Queen Elizabeth II eased her mother's pain in gentle, tactful ways. Under the Regency Act she was made once again Counsellor of State, able to stand in on many occasions for the Queen, who now had an immensely heavy schedule of travels ahead. Queen Elizabeth II had a new set of despatch boxes made for her mother: she was not to be excluded from matters of state. It was announced that she was to be called "Queen Elizabeth The Queen Mother" and, just as the Princesses Elizabeth and Margaret had curtseyed to their grandmother Queen Mary but not, except on the day of his accession, to their own father, Charles and Anne — and the grandchildren who came later — curtseyed to the Queen Mother but not to the Queen herself.

Devotion to family had been the Queen Mother's ruling passion. She had soon to face the greatest family and moral crisis since the abdication without the strength of the King to support her.

Bereaved of her adored, and adoring, father and bereft of much of the companionship of her sister, now so busy both as Queen and with her own family, Princess Margaret had turned increasingly to the company, consolation and devotion of Group Captain Peter Townsend, who had been on the Queen Mother's personal staff since the King's death. How soon her mother realised the desperate difficulties her daughter was in is not publicly known: but until she was told, she trod the fine line between optimism and the ostrich-like vagueness that had helped her to make awkward moments "disappear" ever since her childhood.

To judge from Peter Townsend's own memoirs, she maintained an outward inscrutability when faced with open revelation. She listened, he recounted, "with characteristic understanding . . . without a sign that she felt angered or outraged — or that she acquiesced . . . She never once hurt either of us throughout the whole difficult affair."

But she was herself deeply hurt.

When she told her household in 1953 that Princess Margaret and Group Captain Townsend hoped to marry, she burst into tears in front of them for the only time in her life. Elsewhere she put on an impassive front, as before. But, as Cynthia Asquith had once noted, "Though she may fight with masked batteries her purpose is almost always fulfilled."

She believed the marriage would be wrong in both religious and constitutional terms. To make matters worse her brother-in-law, the Duke of Windsor, was still alive and wounds were reopened by the memories of 1936 and 1937, events that perhaps had helped to precipitate her husband's death. Now she threw all her energies into forestalling what she perceived as another disaster — and perhaps the crisis revived her strength.

A formidable array of advisers had been drawn up to encourage her own marriage to Bertie; now a formidable array, including the Archbishop of Canterbury and the Marquis of Salisbury, was found to discourage Princess Margaret. The past, constitutional reasons, the future, financial and social consequences were all cited — a heavy weight on the conscience of a 23-year-old girl who had led a sheltered life and had always found her greatest support in her home.

It took the Princess two-and-a-half years to reach her painful decision, and to announce to the world, "I have decided not to marry Group Captain Townsend".

"A great act of self-sacrifice," noted Harold Nicolson. The Queen Mother must have rejoiced. Little could she know that this brave, if cruelly hard decision, would open the door to greater unhappiness.

When Antony Armstrong-Jones entered her daughter's life in the late 1950s, the Queen Mother was delighted. The couple shared wit, emotional intensity, artistic talent, a taste for a mixture of high life and Bohemian relief. They married on May 6, 1960, and in 1961 Tony was created Earl of Snowdon, a month before his son David, Viscount Linley, was born. In 1964 Lady Sarah Armstrong-Jones was born, making the Queen Mother grandmother of two sets of "mixed doubles".

It seemed ideal — but not for long. The Queen Mother's hopes of seeing the volatile Princess live perpetually in the state of high-spirits of which she was sometimes capable were doomed to disappointment, though again she seems to have avoided admitting the worst to herself until the fatal blow fell, with the official separation of the couple in 1976 after great and publicly-displayed unhappiness.

The divorce decree, in 1978, that followed two years of separation must have been a bitter blow: yet it forced the Queen Mother, at 78, to reconsider her priorities and to give love and loyalty where it still belonged — to her daughter. They drove together in an open landau to the Trooping the Colour. After the divorce she re-established good relations with her former son-in-law and saw much of the Snowdon's affectionate, artistic and talented children, anxious as ever that children should not suffer from others' disappointments. A friend thinks that she became more understanding and tolerant about the difficulties of some marriages; and perhaps she became even more appreciative of the good fortune she had herself enjoyed.

One of the few people the Queen Mother had ever encountered with a personality as strong as her own was Sir Winston Churchill — the only person she had failed to cajole into playing charades at Windsor. It was he who, several months after she was widowed and had moved from Balmoral (now the Queen's residence) to Birkhall on the Balmoral estate, called on her, un-invited, during a visit to Scotland. He convinced her that she still had much to contribute to life and, plainly, a duty to do so. "That valiant woman," as he called her, began to realise the truth: her country and its many interests, as well as her daughters and the rest of her family, still needed her.

Once set in motion, her immense energy and curiosity took over: before long she was President or Patron of more than 300 organis-ations. These ranged from the Burlington Fair and the National Trust, to St Catherine's Foundation in the East End of London (an organisation which promotes Christian learning), the Royal Horticultural Society, the Aberdeen Angus Society, and her family "Bowes Museum". Her varied interests, so clearly reflected in the sweep of her public duties, were rooted in her home life and personal tastes. Her collection of Chelsea china, much of it given to her as presents by the King, was famous; he also gave her many fireplaces, another of her loves and a symbol to her of the happy homelife she remembered at Glamis.

Now she acquired the first home of her very own, with no memories to remind her of the King. She bought the 11th-century Castle of Mey on the northern tip of Scotland which she had first seen four months after his death while staying with friends near John O'Groats. It was almost derelict. Depending on the weather it could look bleak; or it could provide a marvellous view of the Orkneys. It cried out for nurturing — and a new roof to shelter its inmates — and had wonderful potential. As more royal children were born Birkhall had become too small to accommodate them all, even though a caravan was used as an overflow before more rooms were built on. After much work, the Castle of Mey, the only castle in that part of Scotland, became her favourite place for entertaining her friends and her family.

The castle's magnificent views, ex-quisite tapestry in the drawing room, welcoming fireplace with beautiful mirror above, soft yellow furnishings and — as everywhere in Queen Elizabeth The Queen Mother's homes — an abundance of flowers, indoors and out, revealed that part of her character which loved colour, perfume, warmth, beauty and, when possible, a touch of luxury.

There was also a vegetable garden, and, on the estate, she demonstrated her abilities as countrywoman and businesswoman. She sold a herd of Luing cattle and bought some 30 Aberdeen Angus, and a flock of Cheviot sheep. "She goes to bull sales in Perth and the herd is not purely ornamental — it's commercial," said one friend. "She is rung up constantly about different animals." A farming expert who once showed her round a leasing was deeply impressed by her questions, "Very pertinent: about configuration, and whether they were early calvers and so on." In 1982 she travelled by train to attend the Perth October Show, where one of the bulls from the Castle of Mey was adjudged a "very worthy Reserve Junior Champion" and it was reported that "her enthusiasm and interest in the breed was never more apparent".

She usually flew to Scotland, visit-ing Mey perhaps three times a year as well as Balmoral. Heli-copters and jets alike appealed to her. She completed the first "royal" round-the-world flight in 1978 and on one of her frequent trips abroad she once took the controls of a Comet as the Captain gave it extra throttle. It began to porpoise. Sir Miles Thomas, Chairman of BOAC, said long afterwards, "I still shudder every time I think of that flight."

Arriving quickly — often with two reluctant corgis who were inclined to seek refuge underneath aircraft — appealed to her; but on arrival she was all for her usual leisurely pace, and gentle pursuits.

She was a member of the Women's Institute — and was at one time, with Queen Mary, joint President — and was known for taking an interest in Scotland in such local events as fêtes, flower shows, sheepdog, trials and above all, fishing. For this she wore clothes that showed a very different side of her character from that displayed by the ornate ballgowns she was famed for in her prime, and that suited her even in her 80s, when she often chose silver brocades to set off her hair and complexion. For standing for hours in the River Thurso she would wear trousers, waders, and one of "my dear, dreadful old felt hats". Her skill with the salmon was famed at Balmoral and fly fishing was one of the more visible talents she passed on to her first grandchild, Prince Charles.

Her protection of him and ability to keep him amused as a child were seen at the Coronation in 1953 when he was four years old. At taxing moments in the ceremony she intro-duced him to the mysteries of her handbag. When he was enduring the first agonies as an adolescent prince at Gordonstoun, it was she who light-ened his miseries by making sure he could be with her on his occasional free weekends. As he grew older and had to endure the mortification of being "different", and then the dawning worry of his deep future responsibilities, she saw in him much of her husband and said, "He is a very gentle boy, with a very kind heart, which I think is the essence of everything" — words that revealed her own essential sympathy.

After the shock of the sudden death of her beloved brother Sir David Bowes-Lyon, aged 59, while he was staying with her in Scotland in 1961, she not only comforted Charles, but in turn sought from him consola-tion and company. The death of her sister Rose in 1967 left her as the sole survivor of her generation; now she looked for the family qualities in the younger ones. In Prince Andrew she saw a reflection of her own buoyancy, in Princess Anne King George's enormous courage, in Prince Edward sweetness and a quiet determination, in Princess Margaret and her children the artistic sense she had known in her mother, in Charles not only a dedicated future King but a warm companion and friend.

Her love of painting as a living art prompted her decision to include stained glass windows by John Piper in the King George VI Memorial Chapel at Windsor; it was Piper who had been commissioned to record Windsor Castle in watercolour during the war in case it was destroyed. She had a fine collection of paintings from which she lent some examples to the Queen's Gallery for her daughter's Silver Jubilee exhibition in 1977. These included a portrait of George Bernard Shaw by Augustus John, one of her favourites (she had an un-finished portrait of herself by him), a Paul Nash landscape, paintings by Monet and Sisley and her friend Edward Seago. The surveyor of the

Queen's pictures, Sir Oliver Millar, has been quoted as saying that the Queen Mother's taste revealed "an instinctive delight in sheer quality of good or attractive painting which has not perhaps been seen in the collection's history since the death of George IV . . ."

Ever eager to break new ground, in 1978 the Queen Mother became the first female Warden of the Cinque Ports. Her stamina in carrying out her duties astounded those who did not know her well. In the same year, historian and author Peter Lane was told that in the public sphere, "without doubt her main interest now is London University". She had become its Chancellor in 1955, a position she held for 25 years until she retired soon after she was 80. No figurehead, at a degree-giving ceremony in the 1970s, she bowed to each of 1,985 new graduates and the lady-in-waiting behind her (and five years younger) felt "absolutely giddy".

Harold Nicolson conveyed the aura she created when she opened the new buildings of Morley College in Lambeth in 1958: "She was in her best mood and spirits . . . You know how much I like people who are good at their jobs . . . and she is superb at *her* job. Somehow she creates such an impression of goodwill and good behaviour . . ."

When one President of the London University Union took the floor with her to open the University Ball, his waltz practised to perfection, the shock of a foxtrot stopped him in his tracks. "I can't do it," he said flatly. "Oh don't worry", responded his partner, gaily, "neither can I."

"She's very clever," commented another Union President. "She gives the impression of being nervous, and puts you at your ease."

That same ability to instil confidence in strangers as well as husband and grandchildren was displayed in her chief private relaxation, the sport of kings, horse racing. One of her jockeys said, "She has a very calming effect." She took to horse racing late (when she and the then Princess Elizabeth bought a steeplechaser in an attempt to divert themselves and their emotions from unremitting anxiety about the King's illness). She later went on as sole owner to steeplechase under her own Strathmore colours. At one time she had 15 horses and as many winners each season; by 1983 she had only half-a-dozen steeplechasers and would expect perhaps 10 wins or so. Whatever the weather she went to the paddock to talk to her jockeys — she made them look tall —

and such was her sympathy for them that when her favoured horse *Devon Loch* spreadeagled while leading on the home straight in the 1956 Grand National she immediately went to comfort Dick Francis, who had been up, and the stable lads. Hers not to seek solace, nor to reason why, but to console.

Such was her interest that, though the excitement of the unpredictable in a regulated life was probably the sport's main attraction for her, she nevertheless often watched the last three furlongs over again in the camera room. And fully aware of the tragedies that can follow a fall, particularly over the sticks, she became Patron of the Injured Jockeys Fund (and of the National Hunt Committee).

Ascot week was without doubt one of her favourites in the year: a chance to combine her love of racing with her indulgence in dressing up to please the crowd and, in the evenings, to enjoy the social life of her beloved Windsor in one of its festive moods.

Yet the Royal Lodge at Windsor, near the Castle which had become the family venue for Christmas (Sandringham had been outgrown by the family firm now that it had expanded from four to more than a score), remained her favourite retreat for most weekends, except when she was in Scotland. Princess Margaret and her children often stayed there with her, and Sunday morning service at the chapel was normally followed by pre-luncheon drinks at the Royal Lodge, at which the whole family and any guests would gather, the hostess herself usually in sparkling mood.

It was after a late-night supper with family and friends at Windsor that she was driven some 30 miles to London for an operation to remove a salmon bone from her throat in the early hours of Monday, November 22, 1982. Within 48 hours she was home. A hospital spokesman commented, "For a woman her age, her constitution is quite remarkable." So was her acumen. Capable, as always, of smothering an incipient rumour at birth, she emerged on the steps of King Edward VII hospital wearing a powder-blue dress and coat that revealed an unscarred throat, bare except for her favourite daytime jewelry, a triple row of pearls. A flattering "spotted" veil and a warm smile completed the impression of still-radiant femininity.

Never having dieted rigidly had helped to keep her flesh fairly firm. She disliked both oysters and caviar but had a weakness for other fish dishes in exquisite French sauces, for the fine wines she had learnt about

from her father, and for chocolates, in which she seemed to enjoy an almost wilful indulgence. At the races she was not averse to the warming effect of a pink gin, while at morning engagements a gin and Dubonnet was notified by circular as a good drink for her hosts to offer, even if she chose not to accept it.

Even after the "fishbone" operation she refused, according to those around her, to rest in the afternoons. It was not her first experience of surgery since an obstruction in 1966 had necessitated a colostomy. But she had a spartan dislike of her own illnesses, and though most winters she suffered from two heavy, bronchial, colds she would leave her sickroom as rapidly as the thermometer permitted.

In her 80s the pace set for her was a little slower. Previously her programme would have been booked up two years ahead: now it was only sketched in for several months at a time. Her memory for faces was less instant, but she still showed the same deep interest in their owners: "It was so nice to hear that you can dance and walk the dog," she said to a six-year-old blind girl at the Children of Courage Awards on December 15, 1982, and, knowing that the child's favourite TV programme featured Rod Hull and Emu added, "What a pity Emu can't be here in Westminster Abbey."

Her own courage had resulted in her attending an evening meeting at the Royal College of Obstetricians and Gynaecologists on November 30, just eight days after her throat operation. The weight and width of her schedule at this time can be judged by what had to be cancelled in those few days — a concert on November 23, a visit to a hospice followed by a visit to the Royal Academy on November 24, a tour of a biscuit factory on November 25, a meeting of the London branch of the Black Watch reunion on November 26 . . . Small wonder that she came top in a survey on the Royal Family as "best at carrying out public duties".

She had shown courage of a different kind in July, 1982, on the day when two bombs were detonated by the IRA killing soldiers riding through Hyde Park and on the bandstand in Regents Park. Devastated by the event — and one of the dead was known to her — she carried on as hostess at a luncheon at Clarence House with outward composure and her usual charm. That same ability to hide her feelings of distress or disappointment in front of guests and hosts, learned as a child, smoothed meetings with the presidents of countries ranging from African nations — some of which she felt had been given independence too quickly — to some in Europe, where, when she visited regimes less appealing to her than they had been previously, she captivated her audience.

"She is very, very good at disguise," said someone close to her, in 1983. "She loves to keep secrets and not to tell anyone her plans. Sometimes this can make things very difficult for those around her" — and sometimes it made them easy.

Deeply conservative at heart — much more so than her daughter Queen Elizabeth II — in her 80s the Queen Mother enjoyed the company of such elder statesmen as former Prime Ministers Macmillan and Lord Home. She preferred the company, outside her family, of men to women; yet a woman of character, such as Dame Freya Stark, could be counted among her most admired friends.

At least once a month she liked to have a luncheon party at Clarence House — and when it was warm enough this was served in the garden, just as it had been when the King was alive. When not formally entertaining she still enjoyed the company of several people at lunch, responding to the stimulus of the day's news, and several members of her Household were always present for this most talkative meal of the day.

In the evening she was less gregarious. Duty might call her from the cosiness of Clarence House into the bleak winter or sometimes chilly summer evenings, but she increasingly enjoyed relaxing in the comfort of her home surroundings. If she wanted to see a film her private cinema in Clarence House could provide it; but more often she was happy to relax with scrambled eggs or some other light dish on a tray in front of the television, watching the day's racing highlights and perhaps some of her favourite programmes — *Steptoe and Son, All Gas and Gaiters,* and *Dad's Army* were among these as were, later, *To the Manor Born* and *Yes, Minister.*

If she was with someone she enjoyed talking late — especially if there were a party or some dancing involved. Yet, "no matter how late she has been up the night before — one o'clock, three o'clock — she is still called at the same time each morning: 7.30," said a member of her household in 1983. "She has immense stamina. I think this can be attributed to two main causes. She has a wonderful

digestion and she sleeps frightfully well — she is amazed that anyone else has to take sleeping pills."

And, though publicly eschewing knowledge of many other less private matters, this observer surmised, "I'm sure she would never get up or go to bed without saying her prayers." One has visions of Christopher Robin kneeling beside her.

Certainly in her later years, she must have realised that, age not withstanding, she had much to be thankful for. Her glorious 80th birthday on August 4, 1980, was marked by a visit to her favourite ballet, and the most charming pictures ever taken of her with her two daughters, beside her. In 1981 Prince Charles's marriage brought a resurgence of royal feeling to the whole of her country. It also brought out her own sympathy for the new Princess of Wales, and sadness that the preparation for such a tremendous task was so different from the training she, and others like her, had undergone. She was horrified at the inroads into privacy that now accompanied the Royal Family's renaissance in public acclaim. The birth of her second great-grandson was the highlight of 1982 — he was christened on her own birthday, August 4, 1982. It was also a year during which she had experienced the fear of having a grandson, Prince Andrew, flying a helicopter on active service in the Falklands War.

She had the great excitement of seeing Princess Margaret's children pursuing their different careers at Camberwell School of Art and in making — and exhibiting — furniture as beautiful as some of her own treasured antiques. She had the affection and companionship of her two daughters. She advised them when possible on private and family affairs;

and also, sometimes, still acted as a counsellor whose continuity with the past and whose infinite tact enabled her to decide not only how small difficulties should be smoothed over, and what should be the emphasis of the Christmas broadcast made nearly every year by the Queen, but also sometimes to assist with the broader matters of State.

She was loved by her family, not only as mother, grandmother and so on, but also as a confidante and, above all, a friend in her own right — a position that is never inherited but always earned. Her life, her timetable — up early, hours of training and dress-fittings, public performances and late nights — still resembled those of a highly-disciplined ballet dancer. She also had the fighting spirit of the prima ballerina. "It may take longer to get the adrenalin flowing," said one friend, "but when she goes into battle she still achieves her purpose."

The greatest tributes came to her, as they should, in her lifetime, and from those who knew her best. Her grandson Charles, Prince of Wales, with his own future Monarchy to contemplate, said of her, "Ever since I can remember, my grandmother has been the most wonderful example of fun, laughter, warmth, infinite security . . . For me she has been one of those extraordinarily rare people whose touch can turn everything to gold."

For his sake, as for his grandfather the King's, she had sometimes secretly been prepared to join battle, Scottish temperament to the fore. Like grandfather, like grandson; one is reminded of King George VI's words to his newly-married daughter, then Princess Elizabeth, about "Mummy, who as you know is the most marvellous person in the world in my eyes".

She represented sweetness, serenity, security and strength to her family. She was also a brilliant representative for them, and for her country. She was, in many senses, a diplomat, the more potent because her purpose was not always revealed.

Yet it was her sweet ways and charm that were applauded. The cleverness that accompanied these was often concealed. She was also, to the end, a true trouper, for whom the show had always to go on.

The pageantry of her country moved her deeply with its symbolism. She knew the significance of her place as a link between past and future, and the importance of remaining staunch. In the words of one devoted follower she was "supremely confident that Britain would come through its present troubles".

Queen Elizabeth II was crowned in Westminster Abbey on June 2, 1953. Above, the Queen Mother in her coronation robes and, left, on the balcony of Buckingham Palace with the Duke of Edinburgh, Prince Charles and Princess Anne after the ceremony. Right, the Queen with the Duke of Edinburgh at Buckingham Palace.

1953

Jan 14 Tito became first President of Yugoslavia

Mar 5 Stalin died, aged 53. The Soviet Leader was succeeded by Malenkov as Chairman of Council of Ministers

Mar 24 Queen Mary, widow of George V, died aged 85

April 8 Jomo Kenyatta sentenced to seven years' hard labour for supporting Mau Mau terrorist activity in Kenya

April 16 Royal yacht *Britannia* launched

Apr 25 James Watson and Francis Crick published DNA double helix model findings

May 18 Queen Mother moved from Buckingham Palace to Clarence House

May 29 First ascent of Everest made by Edmund Hillary and Sherpa Tenzing, members of British team led by John Hunt

Jun 2 Coronation of Elizabeth II at Westminster Abbey

Jul 21 British Press Council founded

Jul 27 Korean War ended by armistice at Panmunjom

Aug 20 USSR announced that it had exploded hydrogen bomb

Sept 12 Khrushchev appointed First Secretary of the Communist Party in USSR

Royal tours: Queen Mother visited Southern Rhodesia and Uganda

1954

Jan 21 First US nuclear-powered submarine, *Nautilus*, launched

Jan 25-Feb 18 At Berlin conference proposals for reunification of Germany rejected by USSR

Apr 17 Colonel Nasser replaced Neguib as Prime Minster of Egypt

May 6 Roger Bannister became first man to run the mile in under 4 minutes

May 7 French fortress of Dien Bien Phu fell to Vietminh forces after eight-week seige

Jul 3 Food rationing in UK ended

Aug 3 Independent Television Authority established

The British vertical take-off aircraft ("Flying Bedstead") made first flight

French writer Colette died, aged 81

Sept 11 Roman Temple of Mithras discovered during City of London rebuilding

Oct 23 West Germany admitted to Nato

Nov 29 Sir George Robey died aged 85

Dec 1 US signed pact of mutual security with Nationalist China

Royal tours: Queen Mother visited US and Canada

1955

Jan 15 USSR recognized independence of West Germany

Jan 17 Britain announced it would produce hydrogen bomb

Apr 5 Sir Winston Churchill resigned, aged 80. Anthony

On May 29, 1953, Edmund Hillary and Sherpa Tenzing Norgay became the first to reach the summit of Mount Everest. The news reached England on coronation morning.

*Right, Roger Bannister [b]
the first man to run a m[ile]
under four minutes. He [broke]
the tape in 3 minutes 59.[4]
seconds on May 6, 1954[, at]
Oxford.*

Top, the Queen Mother with Princess Margaret, Prince Charles and Princess Anne after Trooping the Colour in June, 1954.

Centre, the first vertical takeoff and landing aircraft the "Flying Bedstead" – made its maiden flight in Britain on August 3, 1954.

Above, the Queen Mother visited Southern Rhodesia in 1953.

Left, the Queen Mother on the terrace at Windsor Castle with her dog Pippin.

Eden became Prime Minister
May 14 Warsaw Pact concluded between eight European Communist countries
May 15 Austrian State Treaty provided for withdrawal of occupying forces and restoration of Austrian independence
Sept 22 Commercial television began transmissions in Britain
Nov 9 South Africa withdrew from UN
Nov 17 Community drinking water first treated with fluoride in UK
Nov 24 Queen Mother installed as Chancellor of London University
Nov 26 State of emergency declared in Cyprus following Eoka terrorist attacks led by Colonel Grivas
Nov 31 Princess Margaret announced she would not marry Group Captain Peter Townsend
Dec 12 Christopher Cockerell's hovercraft design patented

1956
Jan 1 Sudan became an independent democratic republic
Jan 19 Britain introduced polio vaccine
Mar 2 Morocco achieved independence from France
Mar 9 Archbishop Makarios deported from Cyprus to Seychelles
Apr 17 Premium bonds introduced in Britain
Apr 18 Prince Rainier of Monaco married American film actress Grace Kelly
May 8 First night of John Osborne's *Look Back in Anger* at Royal Court
May 20 Max Beerbohm died, aged 83
Jun 22 Walter de la Mare died, aged 83
Jul 26 Nasser, new President of Egypt, nationalized the Suez Canal
Aug 14 Bertolt Brecht died, aged 58
Sept 29 Bread subsidy ended after 15 years
Oct 17 Britain's first atomic power station opened at Calder Hall, Cumberland
Oct 29 Israeli forces invaded Sinai Peninsula. Anglo-French forces landed in Egypt on Nov 5 but American pressure forced ceasefire on Nov 6
Oct 31 Royal Ballet Company formed
Nov 4 Uprising in Hungary quelled by Soviet troops
Nov 30 First videotaped television transmission from CBS Television City, Hollywood
Dec 17 Petrol rationing introduced because of Suez crisis (ended May 15, 1957)
Dec 23 British troops completed withdrawal from Egypt
Royal tours: Queen Mother visited Paris

1957
Jan 9 Anthony Eden resigned. Harold Macmillan became Prime Minister
Jan 22 Israeli forces withdrew

From left, the Queen Mother visited Biggin Hill in April, 1955; in July she attended a reception and tea party for Commonwealth visitors at Lancaster House; she attended Crathie Church while at Balmoral in September; in October she took up residence in her new Scottish home, the Castle of Mey, which had taken nearly three years to renovate and modernize; as Chancellor of London University she attended the election of the convocation chairman at the Senate House in May, 1956; and in June, 1956, she visited the Orkneys.

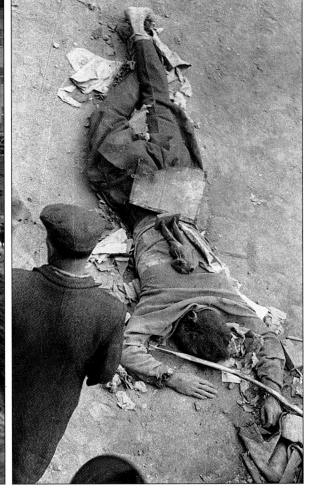

Far left, the first large-scale atomic power station in the world, Calder Hall, Cumberland, began generating on August 20, 1956.

Inset, the Premium Bond was introduced the previous April.

Left, in November, 1956, an uprising in Hungary against the communist regime was quelled by Soviet troops.

Centre above, Christopher Cockerell's hovercraft, seen here in 1959, was patented in December, 1955.

Above, John Osborne's Look Back in Anger opened at the Royal Court Theatre on May 8, 1956, with Alan Bates, Kenneth Haigh and Mary Ure in the cast.

from Sinai

Mar 6 Gold Coast became independent as Ghana

Mar 25 Treaty of Rome established the European Economic Community of Belgium, France, West Germany, Italy, Luxembourg and Netherlands

Mar 29 Suez Canal reopened

Aug 27 USSR announced successful firing of an intercontinental ballistic missile

Aug 31 Malayan Federation became independent

Oct 4 USSR launched first spacecraft, *Sputnik 1*

Oct 21 Queen Elizabeth II addressed UN General Assembly

Dec 19 Regular London-Moscow air service began

Royal tours: Queen Mother visited France; Rhodesia and Nyasaland

1958
Jan 31 US launched first Earth satellite, *Explorer 1*

Feb 17 Campaign for Nuclear Disarmament (CND) launched by Bertrand Russell

Mar 2 British Commonwealth Transatlantic Expedition, led by Vivian Fuchs, completed first crossing of Antarctic continent

Mar 27 Khrushchev became Chairman of Council of Ministers in USSR

Apr 5 Fidel Castro began "total war" against Batista regime in Cuba

May 2 State of emergency declared in Aden

May 29 General de Gaulle formed "government of national safety" in France in response to Algerian war

Jun 1 London Clean Air Act banned burning of untreated coals

Jul 14 King Faisal II of Iraq assassinated

Jul 16 US troops sent to Lebanon and British troops to Jordan to try to preserve peace in Middle East

Jul 24 Life peerages introduced

Jul 26 Prince Charles created Prince of Wales

Last presentation of debutantes at Court

Aug 26 Ralph Vaughan Williams died, aged 85

Oct 28 State opening of Parliament televised for first time

Royal tours: Queen Mother visited New Zealand and Australia (via Canada, Honolulu, Fiji outward; Cocos, Mauritius, Uganda, Malta on return)

1959
Jan 1 Batista government overthrown in Cuba. Castro became Prime Minister

Feb 23-28 European Court of Human Rights inaugurated at Strasbourg

Mar 17 Dalai Lama fled to India after failure of Tibetan rebellion against occupying Chinese

Mar 31 BOAC inaugurated round-the-world jet service

Apr 22 Queen Mother received in Rome by Pope

Top left, Nikita Khrushchev became the Chairman of the Council of Ministers in the USSR on March 27, 1958.

Bertrand Russell, seen above left at a 1961 demonstration, launched the Campaign for Nuclear Disarmament on February 17, 1958.

Above, the Queen Mother was welcomed by Sir Eric Woodward, the Governor of New South Wales, when she visited Australia in 1958. During her tour she visited the Surf Carnival at Manly Beach, left.

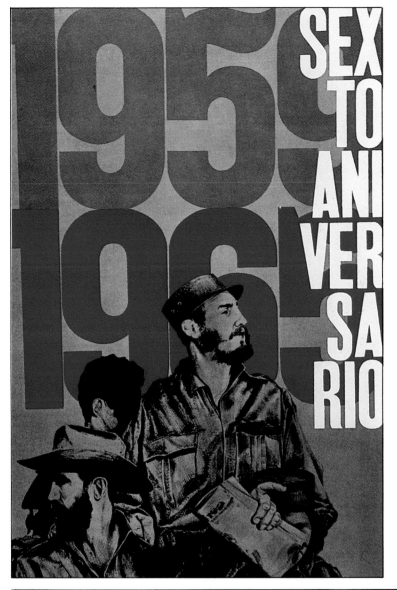

Above left, this 1965 poster commemorates the overthrow of the Batista government in Cuba on January 1, 1959, when Fidel Castro became Prime Minister.

Top, The Queen Mother and Princess Margaret attended a special performance of The Horse's Mouth at the Empire Theatre, Leicester Square, in February, 1959. In April the same year they visited Rome where they attended a reception at the British Embassy, above. They are seen, left, arriving at the Vatican for an audience with Pope John XXIII.

John XXIII
Jul 4 Alaska became 49th American state
Jul 17 Skull of 600,000-year-old "Nutcracker Man" discovered in Tanganyika by Dr Leakey
Jul 25 British hovercraft crossed Channel in 2 hours
Aug 16 Street Offences Act prohibited prostitutes from public soliciting
Aug 19 Jacob Epstein died, aged 78
Aug 21 Hawaii became 50th American state
Aug 26 Morris Mini Minor ("Mini") launched
Sept 13 Soviet spaceship *Luna 2* hit Moon
Nov 1 First section of M1 motorway opened
Nov 10 Emergency in Kenya ended after eight years
Nov 20-29 European Free Trade Association provided trading links among Austria, Britain, Denmark, Norway, Portugal, Sweden and Switzerland
Royal tours: Queen Mother visited Kenya and Uganda

1960

Feb 3 Macmillan's "wind of change" speech delivered to South African Parliament in Cape Town
Feb 13 France exploded first atomic bomb in Sahara
Feb 17 US and Britain agreed to build ballistic missile early-warning station at Fylingdales Moor, Yorks
Feb 19 A second son, Prince Andrew, born to Queen Elizabeth II
Mar 21 67 killed when police fired on anti-apartheid demonstrations at Sharpeville, South Africa
May 1 Soviet ground-to-air missiles shot down American U2 spy plane piloted by Gary Powers
May 6 Princess Margaret married Antony Armstrong-Jones
Jun 30 Congo became independent
Jul 7 First laser operated successfully
Jul 11 Civil war in Congo followed secession of Katanga province
Aug 16 Cyprus became independent under Presidency of Archbishop Makarios
Sept 19 Traffic wardens began duties in London
Oct 1 Nigeria became independent
Oct 21 Britain's first nuclear-powered submarine HMS *Dreadnought* launched
Nov 2 Penguin books acquitted of publishing obscene libel in their unexpurgated edition of D.H. Lawrence's *Lady Chatterley's Lover*
Nov 17 National Service conscription ended
Dec 31 Farthing ceased to be legal tender
Royal tours: Queen Mother visited Rhodesia and Nyasaland

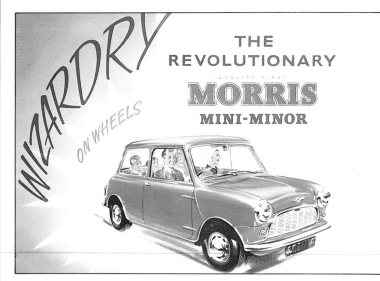

THE REVOLUTIONARY
MORRIS MINI-MINOR
WIZARDRY ON WHEELS

Top, the Morris Mini-Minor was launched on August 26, 1959. During the same year the first section of Britain's first motorway, the M1, was opened, centre.

Above, traffic wardens were introduced in September, 1960.

Right, the Queen Mother attended the Royal Caledonian Ball at Grosvenor House on May 11, 1959.

'MY SPY FLIGHT'

He pleads guilty, is asked about 'suicide needle'

'I was to have used it if I were tortured'

'WERE YOU TORTURED?'—'NO'

MOSCOW, Wednesday. — Yes, I was a spy. I was also a nervous and scared one.

The words were spoken calmly by Francis Gary Powers today as he stood in the chandelier-lit Hall of Columns accused of espionage over Russia in his U-2 airplane.

Hour after hour crew-cut 1960-a-month Powers, looking fit and smart in a navy blue suit, was questioned by Prosecutor-General Rudenko about his mission in May, a mission flown at 68,000 feet, a mission which was stopped by a Russian rocket.

'DETACHMENT 10-10'

"What were you scared of?" quizzed Rudenko. "Just the idea of being over the Soviet Union." It was a reply which brought laughter from some of the 1500 onlookers, who included Powers's wife, Barbara.

The laughter stopped as the questioning switched to the "suicide needle" which Powers carried.

"I was to use it if I was tortured," said Powers.

"Were you?"

"No," answered the flier, who had already pleaded guilty to the 4000-word accusation against him and also admitted that his last place of work was 'detachment 10-10 at Adana Turkey.'

"I was treated very nicely ...

GRINEV (DEFENCE COUNSEL) COURT OFFICIALS POWERS AND ESCORT

Powers, smartly dressed in navy blue suit with dark red tie, glances round the Hall of Columns today. If he knew his wife and parents were there he gave no sign of it.

Morgan Phillips: No change

There was "No change" today in the condition of Mr Morgan Phillips, 58-year-old Labour Party general secretary, it after a stroke. Mrs Phillips was with him for ten minutes. She said afterwards: "The doctors seem to think that there is every sign of my husband making a good recovery. They seemed to be quite pleased with him."

Motorcyclist killed

Motorcyclist John Dennis Alhusser, 28, of Acacia Street, Millwall, was killed when he was in collision with a car in West Ferry Road, Millwall, last night.

WEATHER—Some rain.—See Page ELEVEN

Princess Margaret married Antony Armstrong-Jones on May 6, 1960, at Westminister Abbey, left, and later in the day they waved to the crowds from the balcony at Buckingham Palace, top.

Above centre, the USSR shot down a US high-altitude reconnaisance plane (U-2) on May 1, 1960. Gary Powers, the pilot, whose mission was eventually acknowledged by President Eisenhower, pleaded guilty to spying charges. He was sentenced to 10 years in prison but was releaseed in 1962. Nikita Khrushchev is seen, above, at the United Nations waving photographs taken by Powers of military installations.

1961

Jan 3 Washington severed relations with Cuba

Jan 20 John F. Kennedy inaugurated as 35th American President

Jan 23 Portuguese liner *Santa Maria*, with 600 passengers on board, hijacked in mid-Atlantic by rebels led by Henrique Galvao, protesting against Portuguese regime. It was surrendered to Brazilian navy in Recife on Feb 3

Jan 26 Birth control pill became available in Britain

Feb 5 *Sunday Telegraph* began publication

Mar 14 New Testament section of *New English Bible* published

Apr 12 Soviet astronaut Yuri Gagarin became first man to travel in space, completing orbit of the Earth in spaceship *Vostok*

Apr 17 Cuban exiles, with limited clandestine support from US, made abortive attempt to invade Cuba at the Bay of Pigs

Apr 27 Sierra Leone became independent

May 1 Betting shops opened for first time in UK

May 5 US astronaut Alan Shepard made brief foray into space from Cape Canaveral

May 11 British spy George Blake sentenced to 42 years

May 31 Union of South Africa became a republic and left Commonwealth

Jun 6 Carl Gustav Jung died, aged 85

Jun 8 Duke of Kent married Katharine Worsley

Jul 2 Ernest Hemingway committed suicide, aged 61

Aug 10 Britain applied for EEC membership

Aug 13 East Germany sealed off border between East and West Berlin, and erected Berlin Wall Aug 17-18 to halt exodus from East to West

Sept 17 Dag Hammarskjöld, Secretary-General of the United Nations, died in an air crash in the Congo

Oct 3 Antony Armstrong-Jones created Earl of Snowdon

Oct 10 Entire population of Tristan da Cunha evacuated after volcanic eruption

Nov 3 Princess Margaret gave birth to a son David, Viscount Linley

Dec 9 Tanganyika became independent

Royal tours: Queen Mother visited Tunisia

1962

Feb 25 *Sunday Times* introduced colour supplement

Feb 20 US astronaut John Glenn became second man to orbit the earth in space

Mar 18 State of undeclared war between France and Algeria ended. France acknowledged Algerian independence Jul 3

May 8 Trolley buses ran for last time in London

The Daily

No. 33439. LONDON, TUESDAY, OCTOBER 23, 1962 and

U.S. NAVY TO BLOCKADE ARMS SHIPS FOR CUBA

KENNEDY WARNING ON MISSILE BASES

TASK FORCE TAKES UP

SOVIET CONVOY FOR HAVANA

U.N. report of naval escort

FROM OUR OWN CORRESPONDENT
NEW YORK, Monday.

...ES at the United ...s were discussing ...med report that ...ee days of crisis ...hington may have ...ted by informa-...e Russian convoy ...e to Cuba.

...t time the Russian ...to be travelling with ... This is believed to ...submarines and one ...surface vessels.

...Russian ships have ...y to Cuba. One of ...reported to be a ...0,000 tons.

...ES GOING
...BA BASE

...2,000
...respondent
...Monday.
... are re-
...y to the
...Guan-

President Ken... people last ni... blockade of ar...

WAR RI... RETALI...

MISSILES

...F the American
...v Russia, su
...ates is

Above left, Princess Margaret gave birth to a son, David Albert Charles, Viscount Linley, on November 3, 1961.

Left, betting shops opened for the first time in Britain on May 1, 1961.

Telegr

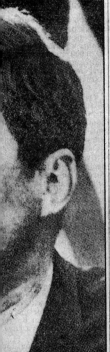

Printed in LON[

PREMIE[
UP THR[
SPY IN[

Opposic[
by su[

BY OUR POLI[
MR. MACM[
swiftly y[
the conviction
Bailey, of [
Vassall 38, t[
clerk, for selli[
Russia [Report[

Within a few [
Minister had a[
Admiralty House [
of a committee of [
Vassall, who p[
four charges un[
Secrets Act, was [
total of 18 years' i[
was said to have [
agents with secre[
the highest import[
of six years.

Sir John Hobson[
General, disclosed [
1957 until Octob[
was employed in [
Civil Lord of the [
Mr. Thomas Galb[
Under-Secretary f[

The inquiry wi[
with all speed by [
three, Sir Charles [
Permanent Under [
Home Office [
Harold Kent, 58, [
tor; and Sir Bu[
Second Secretary [

REFERENCE [
Report before (

It is expected [
Christmas. The [
ence are:
To examine the [
which these off[
mitted with a v[
ing what brea[
arrangements i[
and wh[
neglec[

to the American
d of the Navy's
and of the threat
s.

RUSSIA
BERLIN

MUST GO

TON, Monday.
l leads to retaliation

RMS

Britain for
or the first
ack Indian

cretary, said
the Chinese
The British
traint in the

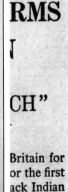

| Washington that America sup- |

Q C Attorney

FOR AMERICA'S

ENTRY

1964

RRESPONDENT
, Monday.
Yacht Club
a challenge
ames Yacht
erica's Cup

ras after a
meeting of
ees, described
a friendly dis-
ous decision."
wn that the
ted a season's
Australia's
st month.
aid the New
ted the chal-
. 1964. "As
ce-commodore
is Septem-

Above, on October 22, 1962, US President John Kennedy announced a naval blockade of Cuba following the revelation that Soviet missile bases had been installed there. The USSR agreed to dismantle the bases and turn back the ships carrying missiles.

Top, Marilyn Monroe died on August 5, 1962, aged 36.

Above, Yuri Gagarin, Russian cosmonaut, became the first man to travel in space on April 12, 1961. He is seen here with Valentina Vladimirovna, the first woman, also Russian, to travel in space. Her flight was made on March 16, 1963.

Right, Adolf Eichmann, a former German Nazi official, was tried in Israel and found guilty of being responsible for the extermination of millions of Jews during the Second World War. He had been captured by Israeli agents in Argentina in 1960 and was hanged on May 31, 1962.

May 25 New Coventry Cathedral consecrated
May 31 Adolf Eichmann hanged by Israelis for war crimes
Jul 1 Act to control immigration from Commonwealth passed
Jul 10 US launched communications satellite *Telstar*, via which first transatlantic television pictures were transmitted Aug 11
Jul 20 G.M. Trevelyan died, aged 86
Aug 5 Marilyn Monroe died in Los Angeles, aged 36
Aug 6 Jamaica became independent
Aug 31 Trinidad and Tobago became independent
Oct 9 Uganda became independent
Oct 22 President Kennedy revealed that Soviet missile bases had been installed in Cuba and announced blockade of island. Crisis was averted when USSR agreed to dismantle bases and turn back ships carrying missiles
Nov 24 First transmission of TV programme *That Was The Week That Was*
Nov 29 Anglo-French agreement reached to build supersonic airliner
Dec 15 Charles Laughton died, aged 63
Dec 18 President Kennedy agreed to supply Britain with Polaris atomic missiles
Royal tours: Queen Mother visited Canada

1963

Jan 29 President de Gaulle opposed British entry to EEC
Mar 16 Soviet astronaut Valentina Vladimirovna became first woman to travel in space
Mar 26 British Consumer Council set up
Mar 27 Beeching Report on British Railways proposed closure of many lines
Apr 9 Sir Winston Churchill made an honorary citizen of US
Apr 24 Princess Alexandra of Kent married Angus Ogilvy, second son of Earl of Airlie
Jun 4 War Minister John Profumo resigned after admitting that he had lied to the House of Commons about his association with Christine Keeler
Jun 24 First demonstration of home video recorder
Jul 30 Kim Philby, British journalist and former Foreign Office official, fled to Moscow after being exposed as "third man" spy
Jul 31 Peerage Act enabled persons to disclaim hereditary titles. Lord Stansgate renounced title and was elected to House of Commons as Anthony Wedgwood Benn
Aug 5 Test-ban treaty prohibiting nuclear weapon tests in atmosphere signed by US, USSR and Britain
Aug 8 Glasgow-London mail train, stopped at Cheddington, Bucks, was robbed of £2.5

million in "Great Train Robbery"

Aug 30 "Hot line" telephone link introduced between Kremlin and White House

Sept 16 Malaysia came into existence by union of Federation of Malaya, Singapore, Sabah and Sarawak

Oct 18 Prime Minister Harold Macmillan resigned on health grounds. He was succeeded by Lord Home, who renounced his earldom and was elected to House of Commons as Sir Alec Douglas-Home on Nov 7

Nov 22 President Kennedy assassinated in Dallas, Texas. Lee Harvey Oswald was arrested and charged with the murder, but was shot dead on Nov 24 by nightclub owner Jack Ruby

Nov 22 Aldous Huxley died, aged 69

Dec 12 Kenya became independent

1964

Mar 10 Elizabeth II's third son, Prince Edward, born

Apr 10 First Greater London Council elections gave Labour a majority

Apr 21 Britain's third TV channel, BBC 2, began transmissions

May 1 Princess Margaret's second child Lady Sarah Armstrong-Jones born

May 27 Pandit Nehru died, aged 74

Jun 5 Britain's *Blue Streak* rocket made first test flight from Woomera, Australia

Jul 6 Malawi (formerly Nyasaland) became independent

Jul 27 Churchill made final appearance in House of Commons

Sept 15 *The Sun* newspaper began publication

Sept 21 Malta became independent

Oct 15 Labour Party won General Election. Harold Wilson became Prime Minister Khrushchev ousted in Russia. He was succeeded by Kosygin as Premier and Brezhnev as First Secretary of Communist Party

Oct 16 China exploded first atomic bomb

Oct 24 Zambia (formerly Northern Rhodesia) became independent

Dec 9 Edith Sitwell died, aged 77

Dec 16 First stage in incomes policy to limit wage rises by mutual agreement signed by Government, TUC and employers

Royal tours: Queen Mother visited West Indies

1965

Jan 4 T.S. Eliot died, aged 76,

Jan 14 Prime Ministers of Northern Ireland and Eire met for first time since partition

Jan 24 Sir Winston Churchill died, aged 90

Feb 11 US President Johnson pledged support for South Vietnam in resisting North

Left, Anthony Buckley's portrait of the Queen Mother was taken to celebrate her 63rd Birthday.

Top, President John F Kennedy was assassinated on a visit to Dallas, Texas, on November 22, 1963, allegedly by Lee Harvey Oswald who was himself shot dead before he came to trial.

Above, Harold Wilson became Prime Minister on October 15, 1964, when the Labour Party won the General Election.

Right, the Queen Mother with Princess Margaret and Lord Snowdon at the theatre in 1964.

Vietnamese aggression
Feb 18 The Gambia became independent
Apr 6 Capital gains tax introduced
Early Bird, first commercial satellite, launched from Cape Kennedy
Jun 11 The Beatles awarded MBEs in Queen's birthday honours list
Jun 17 Commonwealth Secretariat established
Jul 29 Pictures of Mars taken by *Mariner 4* showed planet lifeless and crater-pocked
Sept 4 Albert Schweitzer died, aged 90
Nov 9 Death penalty abolished in Britain
Nov 11 Unilateral Declaration of Independence by Ian Smith in Rhodesia
Royal tours: Queen Mother visited Jamaica and Barbados; Canada; Federal Republic of Germany

1966
Jan 19 Mrs Indira Gandhi became Prime Minister of India
Feb 3 Soviet spaceship *Luna 9* made unmanned "soft" landing on Moon
Mar 10 French Government announced withdrawal of troops from Nato
Apr 10 Evelyn Waugh died, aged 62
May 3 *The Times* put news on front page instead of classified advertisements
May 26 Guyana (formerly British Guiana) became independent
Jul 30 England won football World Cup, defeating West Germany 4-2 in the final at Wembley
Jul 31 Colonial Office dissolved, its responsibilities taken over by Commonwealth Office
Aug 18 Red Guards made first appearance in Peking at mass rally at which Mao Tse-tung initiated Cultural Revolution
Sept 6 Hendrik Verwoerd, Prime Minister of South Africa, assassinated
Sept 30 Botswana (formerly Bechuanaland) became independent
Oct 4 Lesotho (formerly Basutoland) became independent
Oct 21 Coal tip slide at Welsh village of Aberfan killed 116 children and 28 adults
Oct 22 Spy George Blake escaped from Wormwood Scrubs
Nov 30 Barbados became independent
Dec 15 Walt Disney died, aged 65
Royal tours: Queen Mother visited Australia, Fiji and New Zealand

1967
Jan 4 Donald Campbell killed on Coniston water attempting to beat his own water speed record of 276.33mph
Mar 18 *Torrey Canyon* wrecked off Cornish coast causing massive oil spillage

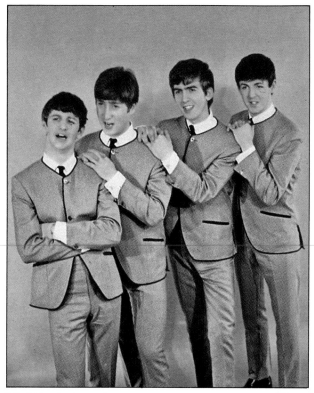

Top, the Beatles were awarded MBEs in the Queen's 1965 birthday honours.

Above, the Queen Mother visited the Ideal Home Exhibition at Olympia in February, 1966.

Above right, England beat West Germany in the final of the World Cup held at Wembley on July 30, 1966. Extra time was played for the first time since 1934 during which England scored two goals. The final score was 4-2.

Right, on October 21, 1966, an avalanche of mine waste slid down a 50-year-old coal tip at the Welsh village of Aberfan engulfing an infant's school, a row of terraced houses and a farmhouse and killing 116 children and 28 adults. The Queen visited the village, right, on October 29.

Apr 21 Military coup in Greece

May 12 John Masefield died, aged 88

May 28 Francis Chichester arrived on his yacht *Gypsy Moth IV* at Plymouth after sailing single handed around the world in 226 days

May 30 Civil war broke out in Nigeria following secession of Biafra province from Nigerian Federation

Jun 5-10 Israel launched surprise attack on Arab enemies, and in six-day war captured Sinai peninsula, Gaza strip and Old City of Jerusalem

Jun 7 First official visit to Britain by Duke and Duchess of Windsor for unveiling of plaque to Queen Mary

Jun 17 China exploded first hydrogen bomb

Jul 1 First regular colour TV broadcasting began in UK

Sept 1 Siegfried Sassoon died, aged 80

Oct 1 Criminal Justice Act which included majority verdicts came into force

Oct 9 Cuban revolutionary Ché Guevara killed in Bolivia, aged 39

Oct 10 Road Safety Act provided for compulsory "breathalyser" tests

Nov 29 British withdrew from Aden, which was established as People's Republic of South Yemen

Dec 3 First heart transplant performed by Christiaan Barnard in Cape Town

Royal tours: Queen Mother visited France; Canada

1968

Apr 4 Martin Luther King, American civil rights leader, killed in Memphis, Tennessee, aged 39

Apr 23 First 5p and 10p coins issued as Britain moved to decimal currency

Apr 27 Abortion legalized in certain circumstances in Britain

May 16 Ronan Point, newly-built 23-storey tower block of flats in East London, partly collapsed killing four people

Jun 6 US Presidential candidate, Robert F. Kennedy, assassinated in Los Angeles

Aug 20 Soviet troops invaded Czechoslovakia to check movement of liberalization initiated by Prime Minister Dubček

Aug 24 France exploded its first hydrogen bomb

Aug 27 Princess Marina, Duchess of Kent, died aged 61

Sept 12 Albania withdrew from Warsaw Pact

Sept 16 Two-tier-first- and second-class postal system introduced in UK

Sept 26 Theatre Act effectively abolished Lord Chamberlain's powers of censorship

Oct 16 Foreign and Commonwealth offices merged

Dec 21 John Steinbeck died, aged 66

Royal tours: Queen Mother visited Denmark

GIPSY MOTH IV
GOAMAN

Above, the Duke and Duchess of Windsor attended the ceremony unveiling a plaque to Queen Mary at Marlborough House on June 7, 1967. This was the first public recognition of the Duchess by the sovereign since the abdication.

Right, the Queen Mother with the Duke of Gloucester at the ceremony, right.

The two-tier postal system was introduced in Britain on September 16, 1968.

Top left, the Queen Mother at Sandown races in April, 1967.

Above, Martin Luther King, black Baptist minister, led a mass civil rights movement in the United States from the middle 1950s until he was killed by a sniper's bullet at Memphis, Tennessee, on April 4, 1968.

Left, Francis Chichester sailed single-handed around the world at the age of 65. He arrived back in Plymouth in his yacht Gipsy Moth IV on May 28, 1967, and was later knighted by the Queen at Greenwich. The 28,500-mile journey was the longest solo sea voyage ever made.

Right, the Queen Mother with Prince Andrew at the Braemar Highland Gathering in Scotland on September 7, 1968.

1969

Mar 2 First flight of Anglo-French Concorde supersonic jet airliner

Mar 28 Dwight Eisenhower died, aged 78

May 12 Voting age reduced from 21 to 18 years

May 30 First crossing of Arctic Ocean completed by British expedition led by Wally Herbert

Jun 8 Spain closed land frontier with Gibraltar

Jul 1 Prince Charles invested as Prince of Wales at Caernarvon Castle

Jul 21 US astronaut Neil Armstrong became first man to set foot on the Moon

Aug 14 British Government authorized use of troops in Northern Ireland following riots between Protestants and Catholics. British Army assumed full responsibility for security Aug 19

Oct 14 50p piece introduced to replace 10s notes

Oct 22 Divorce law reforms made breakdown of marriage sufficient justification

Nov 7 First round of Strategic Arms Limitation Talks (SALT) held between US and USSR

1970

Jan 12 Civil war in Nigeria ended with collapse of Biafra

Jan 16 Military leader Colonel Gaddafi assumed power in Libya

Jan 21 First Boeing 747 jumbo jets went into transatlantic service

Mar 16 *The New English Bible* Old Testament published

Apr 24 China launched first artificial satellite

May 2 US aircraft bombed North Vietnam in first raids since 1968

Jun 7 E.M. Forster died, aged 91

Jun 18 Conservative Party won general election. Edward Heath became Prime Minister

Sept 6 Palestinian guerrillas hijacked and destroyed four airliners

Sept 17-25 Civil war in Jordan put down by King Hussein caused withdrawal of PLO guerrilla units to Syria and Lebanon

Sept 28 President Nasser of Egypt died, aged 52. He was succeeded by Anwar Sadat

Oct 9 Cambodia became a republic

Nov 9 General de Gaulle died, aged 79

1971

Jan 20-Mar 8 Postmen's strike halted mail deliveries for 47 days

Jan 25 General Idi Amin seized power in Uganda

Feb 15 Decimal currency introduced

Feb 23 Rolls-Royce aero-engine and marine interests nationalized

Jun 7 Soviet spacecraft *Soyuz 11* docked with orbiting space station *Salyut*. Three cosmo-

Left, on July 21, 1969, Neil Armstrong, the United States astronaut, became the first man to set foot on the moon. His cautious first steps were watched on television by hundreds of millions of viewers.

Top, Concorde, the Anglo-French supersonic airliner, made its first flight from Toulouse on March 2, 1969.

Above, Prince Charles was invested by the Queen at Caernarvon Castle on July 1, 1970, as the 21st Prince of Wales.

nauts later died on re-entering Earth's atmosphere

Jun 16 Lord Reith died, aged 81

Jul 6 Louis Armstrong died, aged 71

Sept 11 Khrushchev died, aged 77

Oct 25 People's Republic of China admitted to UN, Taiwan expelled

Oct 27 Congo-Kinshasa renamed Zaire Republic

Dec 3 13-day war between India and Pakistan following secession of Bangladesh from Pakistan

1972

Jan 9-Feb 28 Seven-week coal strike crippled Britain

Jan 30 13 civilian demonstrators killed by British troops in Londonderry

Pakistan withdrew from Commonwealth in protest against imminent recognition of Bangladesh

Feb 21 US President Nixon visited China

Mar 13 Britain and China resumed full diplomatic relations

Mar 29 Tutankhamun exhibition opened at British Museum

Mar 30 Northern Ireland constitution suspended and direct rule from Westminster imposed

May 22 Ceylon renamed Sri Lanka

May 28 Duke of Windsor died in Paris, aged 77

Jul 8 Prince Richard of Gloucester married Birgitte van Deurs

Jul 18 Home Secretary Reginald Maudling resigned due to connexion with Poulson bankruptcy case

Aug 4 General Amin announced expulsion of all Ugandan Asians

Aug 26-Sept 10 US swimmer Mark Spitz won record seven gold medals at Munich Olympics

Aug 28 Prince William of Gloucester killed in air race crash, aged 30

Sept 1 Iceland's unilateral extension of fishing limits from 12 to 50 miles precipitated Cod War with Britain
School leaving age in Britain raised to 16

Sept 5 Arab terrorists kidnapped Israeli competitors at Munich Olympic Games. 17 people killed in subsequent gun battle at airport

Nov 7 Richard Nixon re-elected President of USA

Nov 20 Queen Elizabeth II and Prince Philip celebrated Silver Wedding

Dec 26 Harry S. Truman died, aged 88

1973

Jan 1 Britain, Ireland and Denmark formally became members of EEC

Jan 27 Peace agreement signed in Paris ended direct involvement of US ground troops in Vietnam

Mar 8 Referendum in Northern Ireland resulted in massive

Far left, the Soviet Union's spacecraft Soyuz 11 docked with the Salyut orbital scientific station on June 7, 1971. The three cosmonauts on board entered Salyut through a connecting tunnel and remained in space for a further 23 days. Soyuz 11, detaching itself from Salyut, made a perfect soft landing on Earth on June 30 but all three cosmonauts were found dead in their seats.

Above left, Mark Spitz of the United States won a record seven gold medals in the 1972 Olympics in Munich. The Games were interrupted on September 5 when 11 Israeli athletes were murdered by Arab terrorists. Five of the terrorists and one German policeman were also killed bringing the death total to 17.

Above, 50 of the treasures from Tutankhamun's tomb, including his gold funeral mask, were exhibited at the British Museum for six months during 1972.

Left, on November 20, 1972, Queen Elizabeth II and the Duke of Edinburgh celebrated their silver wedding. In this picture are, standing, Lord Snowdon; the Duke of Kent; Prince Michael of Kent; The Duke of Edinburgh; George, Earl of St Andrews; Prince Charles; Prince Andrew; Angus Ogilvy; seated, Princess Margaret; the Duchess of Kent holding Lord Nicholas Windsor; the Queen Mother; the Queen; Princess Anne; Marina Ogilvy; Princess Alexandra; James Ogilvy; front row, Lady Sarah Armstrong-Jones; David, Viscount Linley; Prince Edward; and Lady Helen Windsor.

majority for remaining in UK

Mar 26 Noël Coward died, aged 73

Apr 1 Value Added Tax introduced in Britain

Apr 8 Pablo Picasso died, aged 91

May 25 First of relays of US astronauts docked vehicle with space station *Skylab*

Sept 28 W.H. Auden died, aged 66

Oct 6 Yom Kippur War launched by surprise attack on Israel by Egypt and Syria. Conflict ended after 18 days of fighting

Nov 13 Government declared state of emergency in Britain to meet energy crisis following cuts in Middle East oil supplies and industrial action at home

Nov 14 Princess Anne married Captain Mark Phillips in Westminster Abbey

Dec 13 Prime Minister Edward Heath announced a three-day week in non-essential industries to conserve energy

1974

Jan 1 New Year's Day was a Bank Holiday in Britain for the first time

Feb 13 Nobel prize winning author Alexander Solzhenitsyn deported from USSR

Feb 28 Harold Wilson took office as Prime Minister of minority Labour Government

Mar 7 Three-day week and state of emergency ended

Mar 20 Unsuccessful kidnap attempt on Princess Anne and Captain Mark Phillips in London

May 24 Duke Ellington died, aged 75

Jun 1 29 people died when Nypro chemical plant at Flixborough, Humberside, destroyed by explosion and fire

Jun 10 Duke of Gloucester died, aged 74

Jun 17 Westminster Hall damaged by IRA bomb blast

Jul 20 Turkish forces invaded Cyprus

Aug 9 President Nixon, implicated in Watergate scandal, and faced with threat of impeachment, resigned. He was succeeded by Vice-President, Gerald Ford

Sept 12 Emperor Haile Selassie of Ethiopia deposed by radical army officers

Royal tours: Queen Mother visited Canada

1975

Feb 11 Margaret Thatcher elected leader of Conservative Party

Feb 14 P.G. Wodehouse died, aged 94

Mar 28 43 killed in London Underground train crash at Moorgate station

Apr 30 Vietnam War ended with unconditional surrender of South Vietnamese

Jun 5 Suez Canal reopened to shipping eight years after closure following Arab/Israeli six-day war

First British referendum result-

Top, Haile Selassie, Emperor of Ethiopia, was deposed on September 12, 1974.

Above, Richard Nixon, President of the United States, resigned on August 9, 1974, following his admission that he had withheld information on the Watergate affair.

Far left, Princess Anne was the first of the Queen Mother's grandchildren to be married. Her wedding with Captain Mark Phillips of the Queen's Dragoon Guards took place at Westminster Abbey on November 14, 1973.

Top left, 29 people were killed and the village of Flixborough, Humberside, was reduced to ruins when the Nypro chemical plant was destroyed in an explosion and subsequent fire on June 1, 1974.

Left, the Queen Mother and the Queen visited gun-dog trials on August 21, 1973, and are seen, above, at the Royal College of Music on December 5 when the Queen Mother received an honorary doctorate of music.

ed in decision to stay in EEC

Jul 4 Billie-Jean King won women's singles title at Wimbledon for sixth time

Jul 17 US spacecraft *Apollo* docked with Russian *Soyuz* in joint US-USSR space mission

Aug 27 Haile Selassie died, aged 83

Sept 16 Papua New Guinea became independent

Sept 24 Britain's Dougal Haston and Doug Scott became first men to climb Everest by south-west face

Nov 3 First oil obtained from Britain's North Sea fields

Nov 20 General Franco died, aged 82. Juan Carlos proclaimed King of Spain Nov 22

Nov 29 Racing driver Graham Hill killed in air crash, aged 47

Dec 29 Sex Discrimination Act gave women financial and legal equality

Royal tours: Queen Mother visited Iran; Cyprus

1976

Jan 8 China's Prime Minister Chou En-lai died, aged 78

Jan 12 Agatha Christie died, aged 85

Jan 21 Anglo-French supersonic airliner Concorde went into service, flying from London to Bahrain

Feb 23 L.S. Lowry died, aged 88

Mar 24 Field Marshal Lord Montgomery of Alamein died, aged 89

Mar 27 A 2lb bomb exploded at the ideal Home Exhibition in London injuring 85 people, eight of them children

Apr 5 Prime Minister Harold Wilson resigned and was succeeded by Jamed Callaghan

May 10 Leader of Liberal Party Jeremy Thorpe resigned

Jun 9 Dame Sybil Thorndike died, aged 92

Jun 16 Riots broke out in Soweto and other black townships in South Africa

Jun 27 Palestinians hijacked French aircraft with 250 on board and flew to Entebbe, Uganda. On Jul 4 hostages, mostly Jews, were rescued by Israeli commandos

Jul 7 David Steel elected leader of Liberal Party

Jul 21 British Ambassador in Dublin Christopher Ewart-Biggs killed by land mine under his car

Aug 26 Prince Bernhard of the Netherlands resigned all public posts following allegations of bribery

Sept 9 Chairman Mao Tse-tung died, aged 83

Oct 14 Dame Edith Evans died, aged 88

Oct 25 National Theatre in London officially opened by the Queen

Nov 2 Jimmy Carter defeated President Ford in American election

Nov 9 British Government gave approval to teletext on TV

Royal tours: Queen Mother visited France

Main picture, the first oil from Britain's North Sea fields came ashore in November, 1976.

Above, the Queen Mother celebrated her 75th birthday on August 4, 1975. Norman Parkinson took this birthday portrait.

General Franco died on November 20, 1975, aged 82, bringing to an end the 36-year rule of Europe's last Fascist dictator. He was succeeded by Prince Juan Carlos, who was crowned King of Spain on November 22, and who is seen below with the general.

Right, the Soviet spaceship Soyuz 19 and the US Apollo 15 successfully docked together 140 miles above the Earth on July 17, 1975, two days after take-off. Two of the three American astronauts floated into Soyuz to join the two Russians for a meal.

The US unmanned spacecraft Viking 2 landed on the Utopian Plain of Mars in August, 1976. The computer-enhanced photograph, far right, was taken 261,000 miles away from the planet.

1977

Feb 6 25th anniversary of Queen Elizabeth's accession to the throne

Apr 2 *Red Rum* won Grand National for third time

Jun 7 Bank Holiday to celebrate Queen Elizabeth's Silver Jubilee. State Procession to St Paul's for Thanksgiving Service

Jun 15 First general election held in Spain since 1936 won by Centre Democratic Union

Aug 16 Elvis Presley died, aged 42

Oct 14 Bing Crosby died, aged 73

Oct 18 West German commandos stormed hijacked jet airliner at Mogadishu, Somalia, rescuing 87 passengers and killing three terrorists

Oct 25 Laker Skytrain service to New York inaugurated

Nov 14 First official strike by UK firemen began (ended Jan 12, 1978)

Nov 15 Princess Anne gave birth to son, Peter Mark Andrew

Nov 19-21 Egypt's President Sadat visited Israel and addressed Knesset in peace initiative

Dec 25 Charlie Chaplin died, aged 88

1978

Mar 3 In Rhodesia internal settlement signed by Ian Smith and three Black leaders

Apr 3 Regular broadcasting of British Parliament began

Jun 8 Naomi James became first woman to complete solo circumnavigation of the world via Cape Horn

Jul 11 Princess Margaret and Lord Snowdon divorced

Jul 25 First test-tube baby born in Oldham, England

Aug 16 First transatlantic flight by balloon made by three Americans

Aug 22 Jomo Kenyatta died, aged 86

Sept 17 Camp David agreement on framework of peace treaty between Egypt and Israel

Oct 16 Cardinal Archbishop of Cracow Karol Wojtyla elected Pope as John Paul II

Nov 17 Sea link between Hong Kong and China opened for first time since 1949

Nov 19 Mass suicide of 911 members of American-led People's Temple sect in Guyana

Nov 30 Publication of *The Times*, *Sunday Times* and supplements suspended. Publication resumed Nov 13, 1979

Royal tours: Queen Mother visited Federal Republic of Germany

1979

Jan 1 Full diplomatic relations established between US and China

Jan 16 Shah of Iran went into exile

Jan 22 St Lucia became independent

Mar 1 Referendums of Scot-

Queen Elizabeth II celebrated the 25th anniversary of her accession in 1977. June 7 was declared Jubilee Day and a bank holiday and a Service of Thanksgiving was held at St Paul's Cathedral. Above far right, the Queen Mother is seen leaving the cathedral with Prince Charles, Prince Andrew and Prince Edward. After the service the Queen walked among the crowds near the cathedral, above, and then returned by open landau to Buckingham Palace where the Royal Family appeared on the balcony, right. The picture shows Prince Charles, Prince Edward, Prince Andrew, Lord Mountbatten, the Queen, the Duke of Edinburgh, Captain Mark Phillips, Princess Anne, the Queen Mother and Princess Margaret.

Later that month the Queen Mother and Princess Margaret were at Ascot, far right.

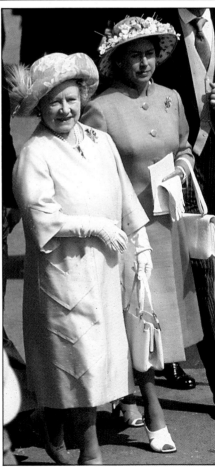

Top, Elvis Presley, the singer, died on August 16, 1977.

Centre, Naomi James became the first woman to sail around the world single-handed in June, 1978.

Above, Louise Brown, the world's first "test-tube" baby was born on July 25, 1978, at Oldham in England.

tish and Welsh voters rejected devolution

Mar 26 Peace treaty signed between Egypt and Israel ended 30 years of state of war

Mar 30 Iran proclaimed republic under Ayatollah Khomeini

Mar 31 Military relationship between Britain and Malta concluded after 181 years

Apr 11 Idi Amin ousted from Uganda by Tanzanian troops

May 3 Conservative Party won general election. Margaret Thatcher became Britain's first woman Prime Minister

Jun 7 First directly-elected European parliament assembled

Jun 12 First crossing of Channel by man-powered aircraft made by Bryan Allen

Aug 1 Queen Mother installed as Lord Warden of the Cinque Ports at Dover

Aug 27 Admiral of the Fleet Earl Mountbatten of Burma killed when his boat was blown up by IRA bomb near Mullaghmore, Co Sligo

Oct 1 US handed over Panama Canal Zone to Panama

Nov 4 50 hostages seized during siege of US Embassy in Teheran

Nov 15 Anthony Blunt, former Surveyor of the Queen's Pictures, confessed to having spied for Russians. He was stripped of his knighthood

Dec 25 Soviet forces invaded Afghanistan

Royal tours: Queen Mother visited Canada

1980

Apr 17 Rhodesia became independent as Zimbabwe

Apr 24 Abortive US commando mission to resue Embassy hostages in Iran. Eight Americans died in helicopter collision during withdrawal

Apr 30 Iranian Embassy in London seized by gunmen. Five days later building stormed by SAS units and hostages freed

Jun 11 NatWest Tower opened in London

Jun 30 Sixpenny-piece ceased to be legal tender

Jul 5 Björn Borg won men's singles title at Wimbledon for fifth successive year

Jul 19 Moscow Olympic Games boycotted by more than 30 nations over Russian invasion of Afghanistan

Jul 27 Deposed Shah of Iran died in Cairo, aged 60

Jul 30 New Hebrides, became independent as Vanuatu

Sept 21 Iraqi forces invaded Iran

Nov 4 President Carter defeated by Republican challenger Ronald Reagan in US presidential election

Nov 13 First close-up pictures of Saturn taken by *Voyager 1*

Nov 22 Mae West died, aged 87

Dec 9 John Lennon murdered in New York, aged 40

Dec 19 Ben Travers died, aged 94

Top, Margaret Thatcher became Britain's first woman Prime Minister when the Conservative Party won the General Election on May 3, 1979.

Centre, on November 4, 1979, 52 American hostages were seized at the US Embassy in Teheran by young Islamic militants. An American commando rescue mission on April 24, 1980, ended in failure when technical faults put three out of eight helicopters out of action. Eight men died in a helicopter collision during withdrawal. The hostages were not released until January, 1981.

Above, 26 people were taken hostage at the Iranian Embassy in London on April 30, 1980. Five hostages were released but on May 5 two were killed and members of the SAS then attacked the embassy, killing five terrorists and capturing one unharmed. The remaining 19 hostages were released.

Above left, in June, 1980, Björn Borg from Sweden won the men's singles title at Wimbledon for the fifth successive year.

Left, John Lennon, pictured here with his wife Yoko Ono, was shot dead outside his home in New York on December 9, 1980.

On August 4, 1980, the Queen Mother celebrated her 80th birthday. Norman Parkinson took the special birthday portraits, above and inset. The Queen Mother was greeted by crowds outside Clarence House on the day, inset centre left, and, later in the month, visited the opera, inset centre right. In June she attended Ascot with Prince Charles and Princess Anne, right.

1981

Jan 1 Greece became 10th member of European Economic Community

Jan 3 Princess Alice, last survivor of Queen Victoria's 37 grandchildren, died aged 97

Jan 20 Iran released US Embassy hostages

Feb 17 Princess Anne succeeded Queen Mother as Chancellor of London University

Mar 26 Social Democratic Party launched by Roy Jenkins, David Owen, William Rodgers and Shirley Williams

Mar 29 First London marathon

Apr 12 Nasa launched space shuttle *Columbia*

May 5 "Bobby" Sands became first of 10 hunger strikers to die in Maze Prison

May 10 First heart transplant in Britain

May 13 Pope John Paul II seriously wounded by gunman in St Peter's Square, Rome

May 15 Second child, Zara, born to Princess Anne

Jul 29 Prince of Wales married Lady Diana Spencer in St Paul's Cathedral

Sept 15 Liberals voted for alliance with SDP

Sept 20 Belize became independent

Oct 6 President Sadat assassinated in Cairo

Nov 1 Antigua and Barbuda became independent

Nov 26 Shirley Williams won by-election at Crosby to give SDP its first elected seat in Parliament

Dec 13 Martial law imposed in Poland

Royal tours: Queen Mother visited Canada

1982

Feb 24 Greenland voted to leave the EEC

Mar 3 Barbican Arts Centre opened in London

Apr 2 Argentine forces invaded Falkland Islands

Apr 4 British naval task force set sail for Falkland Islands

Apr 25 Israel completed final withdrawal from Sinai

May 28 Pope John Paul II began visit to Britain

May 30 Spain became 16th member of Nato

Jun 8 20p piece introduced

Jun 14 Argentine forces in Port Stanley surrendered, Falkland Islands restored to British control

Jun 21 First son, Prince William Arthur Philip Louis, born to Princess of Wales

Oct 11 Henry VIII's warship *Mary Rose*, sunk in Portsmouth harbour in 1545, raised

Nov 10 President Brezhnev died, aged 75. He was succeeded by Yuri Andropov

Dec 10 Soviet cosmonauts returned to earth after record 211 days in space

Royal tours: Queen Mother visited France; Federal Republic of Germany

Top, Princess Alice, last survivor of Queen Victoria's 37 grandchildren, died aged 97 on January 3, 1981.

Centre, the Social Democratic Party, led by Shirley Williams, David Owen, William Rodgers, pictured, and Roy Jenkins, was launched at a press conference in London on March 26, 1981.

Above, in the first London marathon, run from Greenwich Park to Buckingham Palace, about 80 per cent of the 6,700 competitors completed the 26 mile course. Dick Beardsley and Inge Simonsen, seen above, crossed the finishing line hand in hand in 2 hr 11.48 mins.

Right, the world's first reusable space shuttle Columbia was successfully launched from Cape Canaveral in Florida on April 12, 1981.

Far right, the Queen Mother at the Remembrance Day ceremony in November, 1982.

Top left, the Prince of Wales married Lady Diana Spencer in St Paul's Cathedral on July 29, 1981. Soon after their return to Buckingham Palace the bride and groom appeared on the balcony with their attendants and members of their families, top.

Above left, Princess Anne and Captain Mark Phillips's second child, born on May 15, 1981, was christened Zara Anne Elizabeth at the private chapel at Windsor Castle.

Above, the first son of the Prince and Princess of Wales was christened William Arthur Philip Louis by the Archbishop of Canterbury at a private ceremony in the Music Room at Buckingham Palace on August 5, 1982. The Queen Mother, who celebrated her 82nd birthday on the day of the christening, holds Prince William watched by Prince Charles and the Queen.

1983

Jan 17 BBC launched first breakfast T.V programme in Britain

Jan 31 Wearing of front seatbelts became compulsory for motorists in Britain

Feb 9 1981 Derby winner, *Shergar,* kidnapped

Mar 8 Sir William Walton died, aged 80

Apr 21 £1 coin introduced

Jun 9 Conservative Government re-elected with an overall majority of 154 seats

Sept 18 St Kitts and Nevis became independent

Sept 26 US lost America's Cup yachting race to Australia after 132 years as holder

Sept 27 Lady Donaldson elected first woman Lord Mayor of London

Oct 2 Neil Kinnock elected leader of Labour Party

Oct 10 Sir Ralph Richardson died, aged 80

Oct 25 US troops invaded Grenada following military coup on Oct 19 during which Prime Minister, Maurice Bishop, was shot

Nov 14 First US Cruise missiles to arrive in Britain delivered to Greenham Common

Dec 6 Britain's first heart and lung transplant successfully performed at Harefield Hospital, west London

Dec 17 Five people killed and 91 injured when Provisional IRA car bomb exploded outside Harrods in London

Royal tours: Queen Mother visited Northern Ireland; Orkney

1984

Jan 3 Britain's first satellite TV channel opened

Feb 9 President of USSR, Yuri Andropov, died, aged 69. He was succeeded by Konstantin Chernenko, 72

Mar 12 National Miners' strike, which lasted for nearly a year, began

Apr 17 Gunmen inside Libyan People's Bureau, London, fired into crowd demonstrating against Colonel Gaddafi, killing WPC Yvonne Fletcher and wounding 11 others

May 8 Thames flood barrier officially opened by Queen

May 19 Sir John Betjeman died, aged 77

Jun 6 Rebellion by Sikh separatists in the Punjab ended in storming by Indian troops of Golden Temple at Amritsar. 250 Sikhs and 48 troops were killed

Jul 9 Fire destroyed south transept of York Minster

Aug 14 J.B. Priestley died, aged 89

Sept 4 Canada's Progressive Conservative Party won general election ending 21 years of Liberal government

Sept 15 Second son, Henry Charles Albert David, born to Princess of Wales

Oct 4 BBC TV programme drew attention to plight of millions of people in Ethiopia

Above, Australia II *beat the American defending yacht* Liberty *by 41 seconds off Newport, Rhode Island, to become the first foreign winner of the America's Cup.*

Top, WPC Yvonne Fletcher was killed and 11 other people were wounded on April 17, 1984, when gunmen inside the Libyan People's Bureau in St James's Square, London, fired into a crowd demonstrating against Colonel Gadaffi.

Above, fire, believed to have been caused by lightning during an electrical storm, destroyed the roof of the south transept of York Minster on the night of July 9, 1984.

The Queen Mother flew on Concorde for the first time on August 7, 1985. The trip was an 85th birthday present organized by Lord King, chairman of British Airways.

Main picture, the Thames flood barrier, at Woolwich Reach between Silvertown and Charlton, was officially opened by the Queen on May 8, 1984

The second son of the Prince and Princess of Wales was christened Henry Charles Albert David at St George's Chapel, Windsor, on December 21, 1984. Watching his brother, two-and-a-half year old Prince William, are, front row, Lady Fermoy, the Princess of Wales's grandmother, the Queen Mother, the Queen, the Princess of Wales with Prince Henry, Prince Charles and Mrs Shand-Kydd, the Princess of Wales's mother. In the back row, with the baby's grandfathers, the Duke of Edinburgh and Lord Spencer, are Prince Henry's six godparents: Lady Sarah Armstrong-Jones, Bryan Organ, Gerald Ward, Prince Andrew, Lady Vestey and Mrs William Bartholomew.

and other African countries after two years drought and consequent famine

Oct 12 IRA bomb exploded at Grand Hotel, Brighton, during Conservative Party conference killing four people including Sir Anthony Berry MP and Eric Taylor MP

Oct 31 Indira Gandhi, Prime Minister of India, assassinated

Nov 6 Ronald Reagan re-elected President of US

Dec 3 At least 2,500 people killed when methyl isocyanate leaked from underground storage tank near Bhopal in India

Dec 19 Britain agreed to hand over Hong Kong to China in 1997

Royal tours: Queen Mother visited Channel Islands; Venice

1985

Jan 22 Sir Arthur Bryant died, aged 85

Jan 23 Proceedings of House of Lords televised for first time

Feb 4 Spanish/Gibraltarian border opened after 16 years

Mar 10 President Konstantin Chernenko of Soviet Union died, aged 73. He was succeeded by Mikhail Gorbachev, 54

Mar 3 Special National Union of Mineworkers conference voted for return to work

Mar 28 Marc Chagall died, aged 97

May 11 50 people killed when Bradford City Football Club stand caught fire

May 12 New long-runway airport in Falklands opened by Prince Andrew

May 29 38 people killed and 437 injured when fighting broke out before European Cup Final football match between Liverpool and Juventus in Brussels

Jul 7 West Germany's Boris Becker became first unseeded, and youngest, player to win men's singles at Wimbledon

Jul 13 Live Aid rock concert raised more than £50 million for famine relief in Ethiopia

Jul 19 More than 240 people killed when dam burst above Stava in Italian Dolomites

Jul 20 State of emergency declared in South Africa after increased unrest in black townships (lifted March 1986)

Jul 27 President Obote of Uganda overthrown in military coup

Aug 6 Queen Mother flew on Concorde

Sept 2 Wreck of *Titanic* discovered 560 miles off Newfoundland

Sept 19 4,700 people killed and 30,000 injured when earthquake measuring 8.1 on Richter scale hit Mexico City

Oct 10 Orson Welles died, aged 70

Nov 14 Nevada del Ruiz volcano in Colombia erupted killing more than 20,000 people

Royal tours: Queen Mother visited Canada

1986
Jan 9 Defence Secretary Michael Heseltine resigned from Cabinet

Jan 25 Rupert Murdoch began newspaper publishing in Wapping to escape unions

Jan 28 US space shuttle *Challenger* exploded

Mar 4 *Today* newspaper launched

Apr 21 The Queen celebrated her 60th birthday

Apr 26 Soviet nuclear reactor exploded at Chernobyl

Jul 22 Corporal punishment abolished in state schools

Jul 23 Prince Andrew married Sarah Ferguson

Aug 31 British sculptor Henry Moore died, aged 88

Oct 7 *The Independent* newspaper launched

Oct 11 Within USSR Gorbachev expounded perestroika and glasnost

Oct 12 Queen Elizabeth arrived in Peking on first visit to China of reigning British monarch

Oct 27 London's orbital motorway, the M25, was completed

Oct 29 "Big Bang": London Stock Exchange deregulated

Nov 11 Prince and Princess of Wales began tour of Gulf States and Saudi Arabia

1987
Jan 20 Terry Waite, Archbishop of Canterbury's special envoy, disappeared while negotiating for release of hostages in Beirut

Jan 24 Police and pickets injured in clash outside News International plant in Wapping

Mar 6 187 drowned when cross-Channel ferry *Herald of Free Enterprise* capsized off Zeebrugge, Belgium

Jun 11 Mrs Thatcher re-elected for third term

Jul 3 Klaus Barbie jailed for Second World War crimes after trial in Lyons

Aug 17 Rudolf Hess, Hitler's former deputy, committed suicide in Spandau prison, aged 93

Aug 19 Michael Ryan shot 16 people in Hungerford, Berks, then killed himself

Oct 16 Hurricane swept through southern England, killing 18 people, damaging property worth £1,300 million and destroying millions of trees

Oct 23 Lester Piggott, former champion jockey, jailed for three years for tax fraud

Nov 8 11 killed by IRA bomb at Remembrance Day service in Enniskillen, Northern Ireland

Nov 18 30 people died in fire at King's Cross underground station, London

Dec 8 US President Reagan and Soviet President Gorbachev signed treaty banning all intermediate nuclear weapons.

Above, Prince Andrew married Sarah Ferguson on July 23, 1986; after the ceremony the Queen and the Queen Mother were among members of the royal wedding party which made the traditional appearance on the balcony of Buckingham Palace.

Above, The Queen celebrated her 60th birthday on April 21, 1986.

The US space shuttle Challenger exploded on take-off, right, at Cape Canaveral on January 28, 1986.

Southern England was devastated, left, on October 16, 1987 when a hurricane swept across the country destroying millions of trees.

Above, massed tributes to the 95 victims of the Hillsborough stadium tragedy, which occurred on April 15, 1989.

The hand of Diego Maradona scores the winning goal in the 1986 World Cup football match between Argentina and England.

Below, scene of the Boeing 747 crash at Lockerbie, Scotland, December 21, 1988.

Below, the "Herald of Free Enterprise" capsized off Zeebrugge on March 6, 1987, with the loss of 187 lives when water entered the ship through bow doors.

1988

Jan 10 Deputy Prime Minister, Lord Whitelaw, resigned from Government for health reasons
Mar 3 Newly-merged Social and Liberal Democratic Party launched in UK
Apr 10 Sandy Lyle became first Briton to win US Masters golf championship
Apr 23 Michael Ramsay, former Archbishop of Canterbury, died aged 83
May 9 François Mitterrand elected French President
Jul 6 Explosion on North Sea oil platform *Piper Alpha* killed 167
Jul 28 Paddy Ashdown elected leader of newly-formed Social and Liberal Democratic Party
Sep 12 Hurricane *Gilbert* caused severe damage in Jamaica and Mexico, killing more than 170
Sep 24 Ben Johnson of Canada won 100 metres in Seoul Olympics, but was stripped of his medal after failing drug test
Sep 29 US launched manned space shuttle, first since *Challenger*
Nov 7 Prince and Princess of Wales began five-day official visit to France
Nov 8 Republican George Bush defeated Democrat Michael Dukakis in US presidential election
Nov 16 Pakistan People's Party, led by Benazir Bhutto, won election
Nov 29 More than 3,000 people killed when tidal wave hit Bangladesh
Dec 21 PanAmerican Boeing 747 crashed at Lockerbie, Scotland, after bomb explosion on board. 269 people killed
Dec 22 Namibian independence agreement signed in New York

1989

Jan 7 Japanese Emperor Hirohito died, aged 87
Feb 2 F. W. de Klerk succeeded P. W. Botha as South African president
Feb 5 Sky Television, first UK satellite station, launched by Rupert Murdoch
Feb 14 Iran issued *fatweh* imposing death sentence on author Salman Rushdie over his novel *The Satanic Verses*
Feb 15 Soviet troops completed withdrawal from Afghanistan
Mar 24 *Exxon Valdez* tanker ran aground in Alaska, spilling 11 million gallons of oil
Mar 26 First multi-candidate elections in Soviet Union since the revolution. In Moscow Boris Yeltsin beat official candidate
Apr 15 95 people died in crush as football fans crowded into Hillsborough stadium, Sheffield

Jun 3 Chinese Government moved tanks and troops into Tiananmen Square to oust students campaigning for greater democracy

Jun 4 Ayatollah Khomeini of Iran died, aged 87

Aug 20 51 people died when Thames pleasure boat *Marchioness* sank after being rammed by dredger

Sep 22 IRA bomb exploded at Royal Marines School of Music in Deal, killing 11

Oct 9 Queen Elizabeth began state visit to Singapore, followed by journey to Malaysia for Commonwealth conference

Oct 12 Archaeologists unearthed remains of Elizabethan Globe Theatre in Southwark, London

Nov 10 East Germany began to demolish Berlin Wall

Dec 2 Presidents Bush and Gorbachev, meeting aboard ships in Malta, agreed the Cold War was over

Dec 19 US troops invaded Panama to oust General Noriega

Dec 22 Romanian Government overthrown. President Ceausescu and wife executed

Dec 29 Vaclav Havel, playwright and former dissident, unanimously elected President of Czechoslovakia

1990

Feb 2 30-year ban on African National Congress in South Africa ended

Mar 11 Lithuania declared independence from Soviet Union

Apr 16 Actress Greta Garbo died in New York, aged 85

May 15 Van Gogh's *Portrait of Dr Gachet* sold for $82.5 million

Jul 2 1,400 pilgrims killed in stampede at Mecca

Jul 8 West Germany beat Argentina in final of football World Cup in Italy

Aug 2 Iraq forces invaded Kuwait

Aug 4 Queen Elizabeth the Queen Mother celebrated her 90th birthday

Aug 28 Former Guinness chairman Ernest Saunders jailed after 107 days' trial on charges of theft, conspiracy and false accounting

Oct 3 East and West Germany formally reunified

Oct 8 Britain became full member of European Exchange Rate Mechanism

Nov 1 Sir Geoffrey Howe, UK Deputy Prime Minister, resigned from Government

Nov 7 Mary Robinson elected first woman president of Ireland

Nov 28 John Major took office as Prime Minster following resignation of Margaret Thatcher

Dec 2 Helmut Kohl elected Chancellor in first united Germany elections

Left, the tanks rolling into Tiananmen Square in Beijing, on June 3, 1989, were temporarily halted by a single student demonstrating for greater democracy.

Left, demolition of the Berlin Wall began on November 10, 1989, marking the end of the Cold War and heralding the reunification of East and West Germany.

Above, Margaret Thatcher resigned as Prime Minister on November 28, 1990, following the victory of John Major in the Conservative Party's leadership election.

Left, Mary Robinson was elected President of the Republic of Ireland, on November 7, 1990, the first woman to hold the post.

In the course of her journey to Singapore and Malaysia for the Commonwealth conference in October 1989, the Queen visited the Malay College in Kuala Kangsar.

An official portrait of Queen Elizabeth the Queen Mother, left, was issued to mark her 90th birthday on August 4, 1990. Well-wishers stood outside Clarence House, her London residence, to greet her. The occasion was also marked by a series of events. On June 27 a 90th-birthday tribute on Horse Guards Parade involved the service units with which she was associated; and the organisations of which she was patron took part in a procession of floats, bottom left. On July 19 the Queen Mother with Princess Margaret attended a gala at the Palladium, below. On August 1 she sailed up the Thames in "Britannia", toured the East End, and the day ended with fireworks over the Pool of London, bottom.

1991 **Jan 16** Allied forces launched *Operation Desert Storm* to liberate Kuwait following Iraqi invasion
Feb 7 IRA mortar bomb attack damaged 10 Downing Street
Feb 27 Allied forces liberated Kuwait
Mar 19 VAT raised to 17.5 per cent in UK budget
Mar 31 Georgia voted for independence from USSR
Apr 19 Dr George Carey enthroned as Archbishop of Canterbury
May 2 Fighting erupted between Serbs and Croats in Yugoslavia
May 16 Queen addressed joint session of Congress during state visit to USA
May 18 Helen Sharman became first Briton in space as crew member of Soviet *Soyuz* flight
May 21 Former Indian Prime Minister Rajiv Gandhi assassinated
Aug 8 John McCarthy, British journalist held hostage in Beirut for five years, released
Aug 19 Communist hardliners took Gorbachev captive, but coup attempt failed following resistance led by Boris Yeltsin
Nov 2 Australia beat England 12-6 in World Cup rugby final
Nov 5 Robert Maxwell, head of Mirror Group Newspapers and the Maxwell Communication Corporation, died after falling from his yacht
Nov 18 Terry Waite, kidnapped in 1987, freed from Beirut
Dec 1 Egyptian Boutros Boutros-Ghali elected UN Secretary-General
Dec 9 Britain granted opt-out clauses on European Community single currency and social policies in Maastricht treaty
Dec 25 Mikhail Gorbachev resigned as President of USSR which ceased to exist following formation of Commonwealth of 11 Independent States

1992 **Feb 1** US President Bush and Russian President Yeltsin met at Camp David and declared they were no longer adversaries
Feb 11 Mike Tyson, former world heavyweight boxing champion, convicted of rape, jailed for six years
Feb 17 Queen Elizabeth began week's visit to Australia
Mar 2 Eight former Soviet republics admitted to UN
Apr 9 Conservative Party under John Major won UK election with majority reduced to 21

Above, the funeral of former Indian Prime Minister Rajiv Gandhi who was assassinated on May 21, 1991.

Right, 1991 saw the first Briton in space when Helen Sharman joined the Soviet "Soyuz" mission as a crew member.

Below right, the Queen, with President Bush, makes a speech at the White House at the beginning of her state visit to the USA in May 1991.

Below, British journalist John McCarthy was released on August 8, 1991 after being held hostage for five years in Beirut.

Below right, in November 1991 Lord Runcie welcomed home his envoy Terry Waite, who was kidnapped in Beirut in 1987.

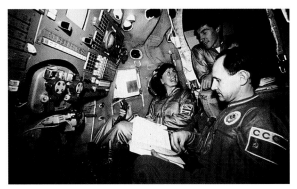

Above, "Operation Desert Storm" was launched on January 16, 1991 by Allied forces to liberate Kuwait from the Iraqi invasion force of Saddam Hussein.

Right, by the end of February 1991 Saddam had lost his self-styled "mother of battles" as the Allies successfully liberated Kuwait and the Gulf War came to an end.

Apr 10 Three killed and many injured by IRA bomb exploded outside Baltic Exchange in City of London
Apr 27 Betty Boothroyd elected first woman Speaker of the House of Commons
Apr 29 Riots in Los Angeles followed acquittal of four policemen accused of beating up black motorist
May 6 Marlene Dietrich, German-born actress and singer, died aged 90
May 12 Queen Elizabeth addressed European Parliament in Strasbourg
Jun 9 Queen Elizabeth began 4-day visit to France
Jul 9 Chris Patten sworn in as Governor of Hong Kong
Jul 18 John Smith elected leader of British Labour Party following resignation of Neil Kinnock
Sep 16 Britain suspended membership of ERM following dramatic fall in value of the pound
Sep 24 David Mellor resigned from Government following revelations about his private life
Oct 8 Willy Brandt, former Chancellor of West Germany, died aged 78
Oct 15 First British troops left to join humanitarian mission in Bosnia
Oct 19 Queen Elizabeth began 5-day state visit to Germany
Nov 3 Bill Clinton, Democrat, Governor of Arkansas, elected US President
Nov 7 Alexander Dubcek former Czechoslovak leader, died aged 70
Nov 11 Church of England Synod voted in favour of ordination of women
Nov 20 Fire damaged St George's Hall and some state apartments in Windsor Castle
Nov 26 Prime Minister announced that the Queen had decided to pay tax on her personal income
Dec 9 Prince and Princess of Wales agreed to separate after 11 years of marriage

1993
Jan 6 Rudolf Nureyev, Russian-born ballet dancer, died aged 54
Feb 12 Prince of Wales began 12-day official visit to USA and Mexico
Feb 14 Body of James Bulger, aged two, was found two days after he was abducted from a Bootle shopping centre
Mar 16 Prince of Wales visited British troops in Bosnia
Apr 3 Grand National declared void after two false starts
Apr 17 At Waco in Texas 51-day siege of the Branch

Above, November 1992 to February 1993, Sir Ranulph Fiennes made the first unsupported crossing of the Antarctic Continent on foot.

Left, after 11 years of marriage the Prince and Princess of Wales agreed to separate in December 1992.

Below, the 51-day siege at the Branch Davidian cult compound in Waco, Texas, culminated in a shoot-out followed by a huge fire in which 87 followers of David Koresh perished.

Below left, in November 1992 a fire badly damaged St George's Hall and some of the state apartments at Windsor Castle.

The 1992 Barcelona Olympic Games saw British sporting heroes bring home gold: Linford Christie, left, won the 100m and Sally Gunnel, below, triumphed in the 400m hurdles.

Three firsts for women: above, on May 17, 1993 Rebecca Stephens became the first British woman to conquer Everest; left, April 27, 1992 saw the first woman Speaker of the House of Commons, Betty Boothroyd; and on November 11, 1992 the Church of England Synod voted in favour of women priests; the first 32 of whom were ordained in 1994, below left.

Bottom left, the Queen Mother attended the opening in July 1993 of the Elizabeth Gate in Hyde Park, London, created in her honour.

Below, on January 6, 1993 the legendary Russian ballet star Rudolf Nureyev died aged 54.

Davidian cult compound ended with deaths of 87 cult members

Apr 24 A photographer was killed, 45 people injured and damage estimated at £1,000 million caused by IRA bomb in City of London

May 3 Viscount Linley announced engagement to Serena Stanhope

May 4 The Queen and the Duke of Edinburgh began state visit to Hungary

May 5 Asil Nasdir, chairman of Polly Peck, jumped bail and flew to northern Cyprus

May 17 Rebecca Stephens became first British woman to conquer Mount Everest

May 20 Queen Mother taken to hospital for operation to remove food lodged in her throat

Jun 10 The Queen visited Northern Ireland

Jun 22 Lloyd's of London announced record losses of £2,910 million for 1990

Jun 28 Duke and Duchess of York agreed terms of legal separation

Jul 3 Barricades erected around City of London to reduce risk of further bomb attacks

Aug 6 Buckingham Palace opened to visitors for 8-week season during the Queen's absence

Sep 13 Yitzhak Rabin, Prime Minister of Israel, and Yassir Arafat, head of the Palestine Liberation Organisation, signed peace accord in Washington

Oct 4 Hard-line Communist opponents of President Yeltsin surrendered after tanks shelled Parliament building which they had refused to leave

Nov 24 Robert Thompson and Jon Venables, both aged 11, found guilty of murdering two-year-old James Bulger

Dec 15 The British and Irish Prime Ministers, John Major and Albert Reynolds, issued joint declaration on achieving peace in Northern Ireland

1994

Jan 7 Bush fires destroyed large areas around Sydney, Australia

Jan 18 Earthquake in Los Angeles killed 57

Jan 31 Britain's Rover car manufacturer sold to German BMW company

Feb 1 Sinn Fein leader Gerry Adams visited New York after visa restrictions lifted

Feb 5 Mortar bomb in Sarajevo market killed 68

Feb 18 The Queen began 3-week tour of eight Caribbean countries

Feb 25 Jewish fanatic killed 29 Arab Muslims in mosque at Hebron

Feb 28 NATO fighters shot down four Serb aircraft defying no-fly zone over Bosnia

Apr 6 Suicide car bomb attack on school bus in Israel killed nine in retaliation for Hebron massacre

Apr 22 Former US President Richard Nixon died, aged 81

Apr 29 More than 250,000 refugees fled Rwanda following slaughter by Hutu armed forces

May 6 The Queen and President Mitterrand travelled through the Channel Tunnel to conduct its official opening

May 10 Nelson Mandela sworn in as president of South Africa

May 12 John Smith, leader of the Labour Party in Britain, died of heart attack, aged 55

Jun 1 South Africa rejoined the Commonwealth

Jun 2 Counter-terrorist experts in Northern Ireland among 29 killed when RAF Chinook helicopter crashed in Scotland

Jun 29 Prince of Wales, in television interview, admitted adultery

Jul 15 Luxembourg Prime Minister Jacques Santer chosen to succeed Jacques Delors as European Commission President

Jul 17 Brazil defeated Italy in final of World Cup football championship

Jul 21 Tony Blair elected leader of Labour Party in Britain

Jul 25 King Husain of Jordan and Israeli Prime Minister Yitzhak Rabin signed peace declaration in Washington

Aug 14 Illich Ramirez Sanchez, known as Carlos the Jackal, captured in Khartoum and taken to prison in Paris

Aug 31 IRA announced ceasefire after 25 years of violence in Ireland and UK

Sep 19 US troops sent to Haiti to restore democratic government

Sep 28 More than 900 died when ferry *Estonia* sank in Baltic

Oct 13 Loyalist paramilitary organisations in Ulster declared a ceasefire

Oct 17 The Queen began four-day visit to Russia

Nov 8 Mid-term US elections resulted in Republicans gaining control of Senate and House of Representatives

Nov 10 Iraq formally recognised sovereignty of Kuwait

Nov 19 First draw in British National Lottery paid out more than £22 million

Nov 30 More than 1,000 passengers and crew rescued from *Achille Lauro* before it sank off coast of Somalia

The Queen and French President Mitterrand, above, officially opened the Channel Tunnel on May 6, 1994.

Left, Tony Blair was elected leader of the Labour Party on July 21, 1994.

Below left, the first draw in the British National Lottery took place on November 19, 1994.

Below, Nelson Mandela, with the widow of Martin Luther King, celebrated the electoral victory of the African National Party, May 2, 1994.

Left, fighting bush fires in the Blue Mountains near Sydney, Australia in January, 1994.

Right, Brazil won the World Cup, July 17, 1994.

Left, the Queen was welcomed by the South African crowds in March 1995.

The Queen Mother drove out from Clarence House in her golf buggy, above, to greet well-wishers and receive flowers on her 95th birthday on August 4, 1995.

American footballer O.J. Simpson was acquitted of double murder charges in Los Angeles on October 3, 1995.

The Queen, Queen Mother and Princess Margaret appeared on the balcony of Buckingham Palace, left, during the VE-day 50th anniversary ceremonies, May 5, 1995, which included a Red Arrows fly-past over The Mall, bottom.

Below, Singapore dealer Nick Leeson, who caused the collapse of Baring's merchant bank, was arrested in Frankfurt on March 2, 1995.

1995

Jan 1 European Union expanded to include Austria, Finland and Sweden

Jan 17 More than 5,000 died in earthquake in Kobe, Japan

Feb 22 British Prime Minister John Major and Irish PM John Bruton launched framework for constitutional settlement in Ulster

Feb 26 Baring's merchant bank collapsed following £800 million losses by Singapore dealer Nick Leeson, who was arrested after fleeing to Frankfurt. On Dec 2 he was sentenced to six years' imprisonment in Singapore after pleading guilty to fraud charges

Mar 9 The Queen paid her first visit to Ulster following the ceasefire

Mar 16 Sinn Fein leader Gerry Adams met US President Clinton in Washington

Mar 20 The Queen began state visit to South Africa

Apr 19 168 people died when car bomb exploded in government building in Oklahoma City, USA

Apr 22 Some 2,000 Hutu refugees massacred by Tutsis in Rwanda

May 5 The Queen addressed both Houses of Parliament at start of 50th anniversary VE-Day celebrations

May 10 UK government ministers met Sinn Fein leaders at Stormont

May 17 Jacques Chirac sworn in as President of France, naming Alain Juppé as Prime Minister

May 24 Lord Wilson of Rievaulx, former British Prime Minister, died aged 79

Jul 4 John Major defeated John Redwood in first-round ballot for leadership of the Conservative Party

Jul 5 Michael Heseltine appointed Deputy PM and Malcolm Rifkind Foreign Secretary following retirement of Douglas Hurd

Jul 11 Capture of UN "safe area" of Srebenica by Bosnian Serbs was followed by the massacre of more than 2,000 Muslims

Jul 25 Seven killed by terrorist bomb on Paris Metro

Aug 31 In UK, August was the hottest since records began in 1659

Sep 5 France carried out underground nuclear test at Mururoa atoll in the Pacific Ocean

Oct 3 Former American footballer O J Simpson acquitted of murder following trial of nearly a year

Oct 9 Lord Home of the Hirsel, former British Prime Minister, died aged 92

Oct 16 First road bridge opened to link Isle of Skye to Scottish mainland

Oct 22 Sir Kingsley Amis, English novelist, died aged 73

Oct 25 Israeli troops began gradual evacuation of West Bank towns

Nov 4 Israeli Prime Minister Rabin assassinated by lone Jewish extremist at peace rally in Tel Aviv

Nov 10 Nigeria suspended from Commonwealth following execution of nine pro-democracy activists

Nov 16 In Britain, *Today* newspaper, launched in 1986, ceased publication

Nov 19 In Polish presidential election Lech Walesa defeated by former Communist Aleksander Kwasniewski

Nov 20 Princess of Wales spoke of her marital problems in *Panorama* interview

Nov 22 Rosemary West found guilty on 10 counts of murder after trial at Winchester

Nov 24 Irish voters approved ending of constitutional ban on divorce

Nov 28 UK budget reduced basic rate of income tax by 1p to 24p

Dec 1 Spanish Foreign Minister Javier Solana appointed NATO Secretary-General

Dec 8 London headmaster Philip Lawrence stabbed to death outside his school

Dec 14 Presidents of Bosnia, Serbia and Croatia signed peace accord in Paris ending four-year conflict

1996

Jan 8 François Mitterrand, former President of France, died aged 79

Jan 15 Andreas Papandreou, Prime Minister of Greece, resigned, replaced by Kostas Simitis

Jan 21 PLO leader Yasser Arafat elected first President of Palestine

Jan 29 La Fenice opera house in Venice destroyed by fire

Feb 2 Gene Kelly, American film choreographer and dancer, died aged 83

Feb 9 Bomb explosion in Isle of Dogs heralded ending of IRA's 17-month ceasefire

Feb 15 Massive oil spill caused by Tanker *Sea Empress* running aground off Milford Haven, Wales

Mar 2 John Howard's Liberal National coalition won general election in Australia

Mar 3 In Spanish elections, Popular Party led by José María Aznar defeated Felipe Gonzalez's Socialist Party

The first road bridge linking the Isle of Skye to the Scottish mainland, above, was opened on October 16, 1995.

Right, hundreds of wreaths were laid outside the primary school in Dunblane, Scotland, where 16 children and their teacher were shot dead and others wounded when gun-fanatic Thomas Hamilton entered the school on March 13, 1996, and fired at a class of young boys and girls.

Below, The Princess of Wales spoke of her marital problems when she was interviewed on the BBC television programme "Panorama" on November 20, 1995.

Left, the historic Teatro La Fenice in Venice was largely destroyed by fire on January 29, 1996. Much admired for its blue, cream and gold interior, the Fenice had ironically risen from the ashes of an earlier theatre burnt down on the site. No fewer than five operas by Verdi had their first performances there, as did works by Stravinsky, Britten and contemporary Italian composers.

Above, serious damage to wildlife and to the environment was caused when the oil tanker "Sea Empress" ran aground on February 15, 1996, off the port of Milford Haven in south Wales spilling 72,000 tonnes of its cargo.

Below, the Arndale shopping centre in central Manchester was virtually destroyed when the IRA exploded a bomb on June 15, 1996, injuring 220 people.

Left, the Queen with King Bhumibol Adulyadej of Thailand during a five-day visit which she and the Duke of Edinburgh made to the country in October 1996.

Right, Donovan Bailey of Canada set a new world record for 100 metres and took the gold medal on July 26 at the 1996 Olympic Games in Atlanta, USA.

Mar 11 George Burns, US comedian, died aged 100
Mar 13 16 children and their teacher at primary school in Dunblane shot dead by Thomas Hamilton, who then killed himself
Mar 25 Export of British beef banned following fears that BSE (mad cow disease) would spread to humans
Mar 31 President Yeltsin of Russia announced ceasefire in Chechenya after 15 months of fighting
Apr 18 97 civilians killed following Israeli attack on UN base at Qâna in Lebanon
May 9 Minority government followed defeat of Congress Party in Indian election
May 21 Tanzanian ferry sank on *Lake Victoria* with loss of 600 lives
Jun 5 Ella Fitzgerald, American jazz singer, died aged 79
Jun 15 IRA bomb exploded in Manchester, injuring 220 and wrecking the Arndale shopping centre
Jul 10 1,000 more troops sent to Northern Ireland following renewed violence
Jul 17 238 people on Paris-bound TWA airliner killed in explosion shortly after take-off from New York
Jul 27 Two killed and 111 injured when bomb exploded at rock concert during Olympic Games in Atlanta, USA
Aug 21 Inaugural production staged at reconstructed Globe Theatre in London
Aug 28 Marriage of Prince and Princess of Wales ended in divorce
Sep 3 US attacked targets in Iraq in response to Saddam Hussein's attacks on Kurds
Oct 12 Jim Bolger remained as caretaker Prime Minister in New Zealand following indecisive elections under proportional representation
Oct 28 The Queen and Prince Philip began five-day visit to Thailand
Nov 5 Democrat Bill Clinton re-elected US President. Republicans retained control of Congress
Russian President Yeltsin underwent heart by-pass
Nov 11 In India 350 died in mid-air collision between Saudi-Arabian and Kazakh Airways airliners
Nov 18 Fire in freight train disrupted traffic in Channel Tunnel
Nov 26 UK Budget reduced income tax by 1p and increased spending on health and education
Dec 13 Kofi Annan of Ghana appointed to succeed Boutros Boutros-Ghali as UN Secretary-General in January, 1997
Dec 29 Last Russian combat troops left Chechenya

1997

Jan 10 Lord Todd, British scientist, died aged 89

Feb 4 Two military helicopters collided over Northern Ireland, killing 73 soldiers

Feb 23 Scientists in Scotland produced a sheep, known as Dolly, by cloning

Mar 22 Comet Hale-Bopp passed its closest to Earth

Mar 24 Tunnel dug by IRA prisoners was discovered at the Maze prison

Mar 25 *The English Patient* won nine Hollywood Oscars

Mar 27 Bodies of 39 members of the Heaven's Gate sect were found in a house in California following a mass suicide

Apr 5 Grand National postponed and Aintree evacuated after IRA coded bomb threat. Race was held two days later

May 1 Tony Blair appointed Prime Minister after Labour Party won UK general election with 179 seat majority in House of Commons

May 6 Bank of England given responsibility for setting interest rates

May 10 At least 1,500 people killed by an earthquake in Iran

May 17 Laurent Kabila became President of Democratic Republic of Congo (formerly Zaire), former President Mobutu fleeing the country

Jun 11 The Queen visited Northern Ireland

Jun 19 William Hague beat Kenneth Clarke by 92 votes to 70 in final round of Conservative Party leadership contest

Jul 5 Martina Hingis, aged 16, became youngest women's singles champion at Wimbledon since 1887

Aug 23 Voluntary evacuation began of Montserrat following volcanic eruptions

Aug 29 Northern Ireland Minister Mo Mowlam invited Sinn Fein to join peace talks

Aug 31 Princess Diana was killed in a car crash in Paris, with her friend Dodi Fayed. The car's chauffeur, from the Ritz Hotel, was also killed, and a bodyguard badly injured

Sep 5 Mother Teresa died, aged 87

Sep 5 Sir George Solti, the conductor, died aged 84

Sep 6 Funeral of Princess Diana held in Westminster Abbey. She was later buried on an island at Althorp

Sep 11 The Scots voted in favour of a Scottish Parliament with tax-raising powers

Sep 18 The Welsh voted in favour of an assembly without tax-raising powers

New eras dawned in 1997: right, in Britain when Tony Blair became the first Labour Prime Minister for 18 years; and, below, in Hong Kong when the former British colony was handed over to the Chinese at midnight on June 30.

Far left, British nanny Louise Woodward, found guilty of murder in USA, October 31, 1997, was later freed.

Left, Tiger Woods became the youngest ever Masters champion, April 13, 1997.

Hello Dolly, February 1997.

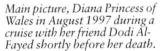

Main picture, Diana Princess of Wales in August 1997 during a cruise with her friend Dodi Al-Fayed shortly before her death.

The late Princess Diana's support of the campaign to ban landmines took her to Bosnia, above left, and to Angola, above right, where she observed minefield clearing.

Left, thousands of floral tributes from all over the world were lain at Diana's home, Kensington Palace, after her death on August 31, 1997.

Below, Diana's funeral and Elton John's tribute relayed to the crowds.

Oct 3 Earthquake damaged the Basilica of St Francis in Assisi

Oct 6 Michael Foale, British-born astronaut, returned to earth after 145 days on the damaged Russian space station Mir

Oct 13 RAF pilot Andy Green drove jet-propelled car at 764.168 mph to break the sound barrier on land for the first time

Oct 16 The Queen's visit to India ran into difficulties because of reported remarks by Foreign Secretary Robin Cook about Kashmir

Nov 14 The US sent a second aircraft carrier, the *USS George Washington*, to the Gulf in response to the expulsion from Baghdad of six American members of the UN inspection team

Nov 17 58 tourists were killed in the Egyptian desert when terrorists opened fire on them with machine guns. Six terrorists and three policemen also died in the gun battle

Nov 20 The Queen and Prince Philip celebrated their golden wedding with a service in Westminster Abbey, a ball in Windsor Castle and lunch at the Banqueting House in Whitehall

Dec 10 Malcolm Chisholm, Minister in the Scottish Office, resigned from the Government in protest at cuts in benefits for single parents. 47 Labour MPs voted against the motion and many more abstained

Dec 11 The Queen attended the decommissioning ceremony of royal yacht *Britannia* at Portsmouth

Dec 16 Sale of beef on the bone was banned in Britain

Dec 20 The High Court upheld a £27 million surcharge imposed on Dame Shirley Porter following the Westminster City Council's homes-for-votes campaign

Dec 27 Ulster loyalist leader was murdered in Maze prison by members of the Irish National Liberation Army

1998

Jan 8 Sir Michael Tippett, composer, died aged 93

Jan 12 British and Irish governments put forward new proposals for peace in Northern Ireland

Jan 25 Queen Mother taken to hospital after a fall at Sandringham. She had an emergency operation to replace her fractured left hip

Jan 26 US President Clinton declared that he had not had sexual relations with Monica Lewinsky in wake of renewed public concern

113

Feb 3 Prince of Wales began tour of Sri Lanka, Bhutan and Nepal
Mar 1 250,000 marched in London to protest at threats to Britain's traditional rural way of life
Mar 19 Right-wing Bharatiya Janata party formed Indian government following indecisive election
Mar 23 President Yeltsin dismissed Russian government of Viktor Chernomyrdin
Mar 25 UK Government proposed elected mayor and assembly for London
Mar 31 UN imposed arms embargo on Yugoslavia and urged talks with Albanian community as fighting began in Kosovo
Apr 10 Good Friday peace agreement signed by British and Irish governments and eight Ulster political parties
Jun 25 Ulster Unionists won largest number of seats in Northern Ireland elections, David Trimble later elected First Minister
Jul 12 France beat Brazil 3-0 in football World Cup final
Aug 15 28 died in car bomb explosion in Omagh, Northern Ireland
Aug 20 US attacked suspected terrorist bases in Afghanistan and a chemical weapons factory in Sudan with Cruise missiles
Aug 23 President Yeltsin dismissed Russian government, agreeing with the Duma that Yevgeni Primakov should take over as Prime Minister
Sep 17 The Queen began state visit to Brunei and Malaysia, where she closed the Commonwealth Games
Sep 24 UK and Iran agreed to remove threats against author Salman Rushdie following imposition of *fatwa* in 1989
Sep 27 German elections removed Chancellor Kohl from office, to be replaced by Gerhard Schroder of the Social Democrats
Oct 18 General Augusto Pinochet, former president of Chile, arrested in a London hospital following request for his extradition to Spain
Oct 27 UK Welsh Secretary Ron Davies resigned following incident on Clapham Common
Oct 28 Ted Hughes, poet laureate, died aged 68
Dec 1 US oil company Exxon announced takeover of Mobil for $82,000m
Dec 16 US and UK bombed Iraq for four nights following Saddam Hussein's refusal to cooperate with UN weapons inspectors
Dec 19 US House of Representatives voted to impeach President Clinton for high crimes and misdemeanours

Above, American singer Frank Sinatra died aged 68 on May 14, 1998.

Left, in January 1998, President Clinton denied having a sexual relationship with Monica Lewinsky; he was impeached a year later on charges of perjury.

Below, on January 1, 1999, 11 EU nations merged their currencies with the Euro.

Right, David Beckham ruined England's 1998 chances in the World Cup by being sent off during the match against Argentina.

Left, in January 1998, the Queen Mother emerged smiling from hospital after an emergency hip operation following a fall at Sandringham.

September 14, 1998 saw the opening session of the Northern Ireland Assembly, below.

1999

Jan 1 11 EU nations, excluding Britain, merged their national currencies with the Euro

Jan 7 Impeachment trial of US President Clinton on charges of perjury and obstruction of justice opened in Senate. He was acquitted on Feb 12

Jan 26 Earthquake in Colombia caused deaths of more than 1,000 people

Feb 7 King Husain of Jordan died, succeeded by son, King Abdullah II

Mar 24 Nato launched massive bomb attacks against targets in Yugoslavia after failure to find peaceful settlement for Kosovo. On following day Serbs began massive "ethnic cleansing" of Albanians in Kosovo

Apr 30 Three died and 73 were injured when nail bomb exploded in gay public house in London

May 7 Three died when Nato accidentally bombed Chinese embassy in Belgrade

May 10 Alun Michael elected First Secretary of Welsh National Assembly

May 17 Donald Dewar elected Scotland's First Minister

May 26 The Queen opened new Welsh National Assembly in Cardiff

May 27 UN War Crimes Tribunal indicted President Milosevic of Yugoslavia of crimes against humanity

Jun 8 Nato ceased bombing Serbia and on Jun 9 agreement was signed for withdrawal of Serb forces from Kosovo and entry of international security force

Jun 9 Former UK Cabinet Minister Jonathan Aitken imprisoned for perjury

Jul 1 The Queen opened new Scottish Assembly in Edinburgh

Jul 16 John F Kennedy Jr, son of former US President, was killed with his wife and sister-in-law when the aircraft he was piloting crashed into the sea

Aug 1 EU lifted three-year ban on British beef

Aug 9 President Yeltsin dismissed Russian government and appointed Vladimir Putin as Prime Minister

Sep 23 Russia launched attacks on separatist republic of Chechenya

Oct 5 31 people died when two trains collided outside Paddington station, London

Oct 11 Peter Mandelson was appointed Northern Ireland Secretary

Oct 12 Pakistan's elected government ousted in military coup led by General Pervez Musharraf

Oct 26 House of Lords voted in favour of Bill to

In August, a car bomb exploded in Omagh, Northern Ireland, killing 28, above.

Left, 250,000 marched on London to defend their rural way of life.

Right, on August 17, 1999, a massive earthquake that measured 7.4 on the Richter scale killed 15,000 people in north-western Turkey.

Left, Prince Edward married Sophie Rhys Jones at Windsor on June 19, 1999.

Right, on August 11, 1999, the last total solar eclipse of the 20th century was witnessed by two billion people.

end voting rights of hereditary peers

Nov 6 Australians voted in referendum to reject proposal to sever links with British monarchy

Nov 25 Michael Portillo won by-election for Kensington & Chelsea seat in House of Commons

Dec 2 Devolved Northern Ireland Government took office, led by First Minister David Trimble

Dec 14 Panama Canal, controlled by US since its opening in 1914, formally handed over to Panama

Dec 16 About 50,000 people died following floods and mudslides along coast of Venezuela

Dec 31 President Yeltsin of Russia resigned, naming Prime Minister Vladimir Putin as acting President. The Queen opened £758m Millennium Dome at Greenwich

2000 Jan 31 Dr Harold
Shipman was convicted of murdering 15 patients and suspected of many more

Feb 1 Russian troops took control of Chechen capital of Grozny

Feb 7 Afghan airliner, hijacked on a domestic flight, landed at Stansted. Many on board requested asylum

Feb 9 Alun Michael, First Secretary of Wales, resigned, replaced by Rhodri Morgan

Feb 11 Ulster returned to direct rule following failure of IRA to start decommissioning. The devolved government resumed at the end of May

Mar 2 Home Secretary Jack Straw ruled that former Chilean President General Pinochet, detained in Britain for 15 months, was free to leave the country

Mar 16 The Queen began two-week tour of Australia

Mar 20 The Pope began six-day pilgrimage to the Holy Land

Mar 26 Vladimir Putin elected President of Russia

Apr 6 Parliament in Zimbabwe passed Land Acquisition Bill allowing white-owned land to be seized without compensation. Later, two white farmers were killed by squatters

Apr 12 The Queen Mother was awarded the citizenship of Volgograd

May 1 Anti-capitalist demonstrators caused widespread damage in London

May 3 Trial opened in Netherlands of two Libyans accused of 1988 Lockerbie bombing

May 4 Ken Livingstone elected Mayor of London

Right, Vladimir Putin, elected President of Russia on March 26, 2000, took tea with the Queen at Windsor in April.

Left, in May, Sinn Fein President Gerry Adams was at the unveiling of a statue to the IRA dead as the IRA announced their weapons would be put beyond use.

Below, the Kursk, *a Russian nuclear submarine, sank to the bottom of the Barents Sea on August 12, 2000, killing all 118 crew.*

Below, Steve Redgrave, 38, won gold in the men's coxless fours in Sydney—his fifth gold medal for rowing in five consecutive Olympic Games.

Below, anti-capitalist demonstrators took to the streets on May Day, spraying red paint on Churchill's statue.

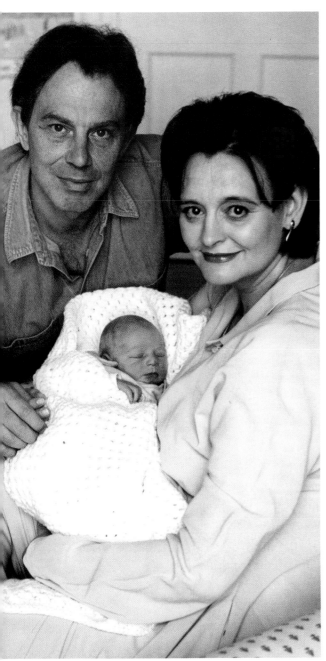

Left, proud parents Tony and Cherie Blair with baby Leo, born on May 20, 2000—the first child to be born to a serving British Prime Minister for 150 years.

Above, Ken Livingstone was elected Mayor of London on May 4, 2000.

Below, American Venus Williams won the women's title at Wimbledon in July 2000.

The Queen Mother in Scotland in August.

Left, on July 25, 2000, an Air France Concorde crashed on take-off from Paris, killing 113 people.

May 8 British troops sent to Sierra Leone to evacuate British nationals and protect airport
May 23 Israeli troops withdrawn from southern Lebanon
Jun 9 Millennium footbridge across the Thames opened then closed when it began to sway
Jun 10 President Assad of Syria died
Jun 19 Bodies of 58 illegal Chinese immigrants found in Dutch truck at Dover
Jun 25 Zimbabwe elections: Robert Mugabe's Zanu-PF party returned with narrow majority
Jul 2 Mexico elections: PRI party, in power for 71 years, was defeated. Vicente Fox elected President
Jul 9 Pete Sampras won Wimbledon men's tennis final for seventh time, completing a record 13 grand slam titles. The American Venus Williams won the women's title
Aug 4 The Queen Mother celebrated her 100th birthday
Sep 12 Garages ran out of petrol as peaceful picketing by hauliers and farmers persuaded tanker drivers not to leave their depots
Sep 20 MI6 HQ in London was slightly damaged by rocket
Sep 28 Denmark voted not to adopt the euro
Oct 1 At the Olympic Games in Sydney, Australia, Britain came 10th in the medal table
Oct 7 Vojislav Kosunica became President of Serbia after Slobodan Milosevic, faced with mounting popular demonstrations in Belgrade, conceded that he had lost the election
Oct 11 Donald Dewar, First Minister of Scotland, died of a brain haemorrhage following a fall outside his official residence in Edinburgh
Oct 17 Four people were killed and 33 hurt when a London-Leeds passenger train left the rails near Hatfield, Herts. Subsequent track inspections and repairs delayed trains and wrecked timetables
Oct 30 Severe storms across Britain caused flooding in many parts of the country
Nov 3 The Queen Mother broke her collarbone after a fall in Clarence House
Nov 7 US presidential election result delayed by recount in Florida following narrow vote between George W Bush and Al Gore
Nov 8 Chancellor Gordon Brown announced a £5 billion pre-Budget package giving increases to pensioners and tax reductions for the haulage industry

100 YEARS YOUNG

The Queen Mother's hundredth year turned out to be one of the busiest and most publicly active of her long life.

Many of the engagements she undertook were inevitably connected with special celebrations for her birthday, including a service of thanksgiving in St Paul's Cathedral, a luncheon at the Guildhall in the City of London where the usual formalities were set aside as guests broke into a spontaneous rendition of the song "If You Were the Only Girl in the World", and a centenary pageant on the Horse Guards Parade. In addition to these happenings, the Queen Mother also carried out a full programme of more traditional royal events, many of them associated with the 320 charities of which she is patron.

Right, as part of the centenary pageant, the Red Arrows flew overhead trailing red, white and blue smoke.

Above right, the Queen Mother, with Prince Charles at her side, rides towards Buckingham Palace in an open carriage decked with flowers.
Above, the Queen Mother leaves St Paul's Cathedral with a helping hand from her favourite grandson, Prince Charles, after attending a national service of thanksgiving to celebrate her remarkable life.

Above, the much-loved centenarian appeared alongside her close family on Buckingham Palace's infamous balcony. Below, the Queen Mother arriving at St Paul's Cathedral to attend a service arranged in her honour.

An appearance by the Queen Mother's beloved corgis, Minnie and Rush, added to the centenary pageant's already jubilant mood, above. The dogs, together with the Queen Mother's steward, Billy Tallon, led a parade of representatives from the 320 worthy causes of which she is president or patron.
Left, mother and daughter greet the throng of well-wishers who gathered outside Buckingham Palace to join in with the Queen Mother's centenary celebrations.

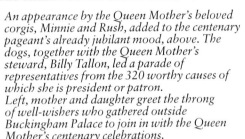

Left, the Queen Mother was joined by 27 other members of the Royal Family on Buckingham Palace's balcony, including, from left to right, Zara Phillips, Princess Anne, Peter Phillips, Princess Beatrice, Prince Andrew and Princess Eugenie.

Above, together with the 13,000 spectators who had packed into Horse Guards Parade, Prince Charles was all smiles as the Wombles, dressed as guardsmen, marched past as part of the Queen Mother's centenary pageant.

2001

Jan 30 Abdul Baset Ali al-Megrahi sentenced to 20 years by a Scottish court in the Netherlands for his part in the Lockerbie bombing of 1988

Feb 6 Ariel Sharon elected Prime Minister of Israel

Feb 19 Foot-and-mouth disease discovered in Essex abbatoir

Mar 28 President Bush confirmed that the US would abandon the Kyoto protocol on reducing greenhouse gases

Apr 1 Former President Slobodan Milosevic was arrested in Belgrade on charges of corruption

Apr 2 Prime Minister Tony Blair announced postponement of local elections because of foot-and-mouth disease

Jun 1 King Birendra, Queen Aiswarya and six other members of the Nepalese royal family were shot dead by the Crown Prince Dipendra, who then shot himself and later died of his injuries

Jun 7 In the British general election, Labour won 413 seats, the Conservatives 166 and the Liberal Democrats 52. On the following day, William Hague resigned his leadership of the Conservative Party

Jun 15 EU Summit meeting in Swedish city of Gothenburg was disrupted by demonstrations

Jun 28 Former President Slobodan Milosevic was extradited to The Hague to face charges of atrocities committed during the Kosovo conflict

Jul 9 Goran Ivanisevic of Croatia won the singles tennis championship at Wimbledon, with Venus Williams retaining her singles title

Jul 19 Lord Archer sentenced to four years in prison on being found guilty of perjury

Jul 20 Anti-capitalist protester shot dead by Italian carabinieri when riots erupted during meeting of G8 leaders in Genoa

Jul 24 More than 20 killed when Tamil Tiger guerillas attacked airport at Columbo, Sri Lanka

Aug 1 Queen Mother given a blood transfusion after being admitted to hospital with a mild form of anaemia. She returned to Clarence House in time to celebrate her 101st birthday on August 4

Aug 3 Car bomb, planted by Real IRA, exploded in Ealing Broadway, London, injuring 15 people

Aug 9 Suicide bomber blew himself up in a Jerusalem

Above, September 11, two hijacked passenger airliners hit the twin towers of the World Trade Center in New York, which subsequently collapsed, killing thousands. A third plane hit the Pentagon in Washington, and a fourth crashed in Pennsylvania.

Right, George W Bush was inaugurated 43rd President of the United States on January 20, 2001.

Centre right, Afghan troops prepare as the US launches its campaign to destroy terrorist bases in the country. Far right, in October, 200 Royal Marines go to Afghanistan.

Above, the Queen with Lord Linley and Lady Sarah Chatto at the funeral of her sister, Princess Margaret, who died on February 9, 2002, aged 71.

Right, the Queen Mother at the recommissioning of HMS Ark Royal in November 2001. This was her last public appearance.

The Queen rides through the grounds of Windsor Castle with Princess Anne and a groom, following the death of the Queen Mother, aged 101, on March 30, 2002.

Below, the Queen Mother's coffin is borne from her official residence, Royal Lodge, into the Royal Chapel of All Saints at Windsor.

pizza restaurant, killing 15 people
Sep 1 England football team beat Germany 5-1
Sep 11 Terrorists hijacked four US airliners, crashing two into the twin towers of the World Trade Center in New York, and another into the Pentagon in Washington. The fourth crashed near Pittsburg after passengers attacked the hijackers. In all, some 3,000 people were killed
Oct 7 US and British forces launched missile attacks on three cities in Afghanistan at start of campaign to destroy terrorist bases
Oct 17 Israeli Minister of Tourism and former general Rehavam Ze'evi was killed by Palestinian gunmen in Jerusalem
Oct 23 The IRA decommissioned part of its armoury
Nov 9 Opposition forces in Afghanistan captured Mazar-i Sharif from Taliban and moved on towards Kabul, which they captured three days later
Nov 12 An American Airlines Airbus A300 crashed in the borough of Queens, New York City, shortly after taking off from JFK Airport. 266 people were killed
Nov 29 George Harrison, former Beatle, died of cancer, aged 58
Dec 6 Sophie Countess of Wessex, wife of Prince Edward, lost her baby after an ectopic pregnancy
Dec 31 Single currency, the euro, came into circulation in 12 European countries

2002

Feb 6 The trial of Slobodan Milosevic, former President of Serbia, began in the International War Crimes Tribunal at The Hague
Feb 9 Princess Margaret died, aged 71, after suffering a third stroke
Mar 10 Robert Mugabe won controversial election in Zimbabwe
Mar 18 British Government announced it would be sending 1,700 Marines to Afghanistan
Mar 19 Zimbabwe's membership of the Commonwealth was suspended for a year because of the violence that accompanied Mugabe's re-election. Sanctions had already been imposed by the EU and the USA
Mar 29 Israeli troops moved into Yasser Arafat's headquarters in Ramallah following more Palestinian suicide bombings in Israel
Mar 30 Queen Elizabeth the Queen Mother died peacefully in her sleep at Windsor, aged 101 ■

CHAPTER 5

THE NATION'S FAREWELL

The Queen Mother had such an enthusiasm for life and ability to connect with the many generations through which she lived that the inevitable sadness in the days following her death at the age of 101 was equalled by many affectionate remembrances, not just of a life lived to the full but one that proved to be an inspiration for the nation.

Queen Elizabeth the Queen Mother died at the Royal Lodge in Windsor Great Park at 3.15pm on Saturday March 30, 2002, peacefully in her sleep with her daughter, the Queen, holding her hand. There was some delay in releasing the news while Prince Charles, who was on a skiing holiday with his two sons, was contacted but, when the announcement was made from Buckingham Palace, it prompted a public response that ultimately became far greater than anyone could have expected.

It started slowly. It was the Easter weekend, there was perceived to be a need for time for private grief within the royal family, and there was, perhaps, also uncertainty within the media about how it should be handled. But, as the tributes and the flowers poured in and the crowds gathered to watch the Queen Mother's coffin being moved from the Royal Chapel at Windsor to the Queen's Chapel at St James's Palace, it became clear to all that

the nation wanted to be involved, not just in sharing the royal family's grief but also in celebrating the life of one of the 20th century's most remarkable women.

This public involvement grew more intense as the day of the funeral approached. On Friday, April 5, large crowds, including some who had camped out overnight, watched as the Queen Mother's coffin was borne along The Mall and Horse Guards Parade to Westminster Hall, where even larger numbers had already started to queue to pay their respects at her lying-in-state. More than 16,000 servicemen had escorted the gun carriage bearing the coffin, drawn by six black horses of the King's Troop, Royal Horse Artillery, in a stately procession more than half a mile long. On top of the coffin, which was draped with the Queen Mother's personal standard, lay the platinum crown she had worn at her husband's coronation, its Koh-I-Noor diamond

Large crowds gathered to witness the procession accompanying the gun carriage on which the coffin was borne along The Mall to Westminster Hall preparatory to the lying-in-state.

Following the coffin on foot were 14 members of the royal family, led by Prince Philip, the Prince of Wales, the Duke of York, the Princess Royal, and the Earl of Wessex.

" SHE WAS QUITE SIMPLY THE MOST MAGICAL GRANDMOTHER YOU COULD POSSIBLY HAVE, AND I WAS UTTERLY DEVOTED TO HER. "

sparkling in the sun, and a single wreath of white roses, freesias and sweet peas with a card written by the Queen and bearing the words "In loving memory, Lilibet."

Following the gun carriage on foot were 14 members of the royal family, led by Prince Philip, the Prince of Wales, the Duke of York, the Earl of Wessex and the Princess Royal, who had been given the Queen's permission to break with tradition and march with the men, which she did in full dress-trousered naval uniform. Behind them came Prince William and Prince Harry, in morning suits, other members of the royal and the Bowes-Lyon families, and members of the Queen Mother's personal staff.

As the procession moved away from St James's Palace, the guardsmen lining the route reversed their weapons and bowed their heads while a gun was fired, the first of a 28-gun royal salute fired once every minute by the Royal Horse Artillery stationed in Green Park until, as Big Ben struck 12, the procession arrived at Westminster Hall, where the Queen and other female members of the royal family were waiting, together with the Archbishop of Canterbury, Dr George Carey. Pallbearers drawn from the Queen's guards' regiments carried the coffin to the catafalque inside the hall, where the Prime Minister, Mr Tony Blair, and other members of the two Houses of Parliament were assembled. Two short prayers were read by Dr Carey, the first giving thanks for the Queen Mother's "example of faithful duty and unwearied service, and for the loyalty and love which she inspired", and the second asking the Almighty to "deal graciously with those who mourn". Four officers of the Household Cavalry then took up position at the four corners of the catafalque, with bowed heads and hands folded on the hilts of their swords, to begin the vigil, which continued, with a rota of officers changing every 20 minutes, until the morning of the funeral.

Of all those present at this moving ceremony, the Prince of Wales was the most

Above, the coffin passes the Queen and other female members of the royal family on its way into Westminster Hall for the lying-in-state.

Right, floral tributes poured in and queues rapidly formed as people waited to file through the hall throughout the days and most of the nights.

"THE EXTENT OF THE TRIBUTE THAT HUGE NUMBERS OF YOU HAVE PAID MY MOTHER IN THE LAST FEW DAYS HAS BEEN OVERWHELMING."

Top and right, the Queen Mother's four grandsons took a turn at standing vigil at the four corners of the catafalque on the night before the funeral, watched by the Princess Royal, Prince William and Prince Harry.

Above, one of the many imaginative tributes left outside Clarence House, suggesting that what was needed at times like these was a stiff drink.

Above, the gun carriage bearing the coffin on its way along the processional route towards the west door of Westminster Abbey.

Right, some of the distinguished guests who attended the funeral. Clockwise from the left, the King and Queen of Spain, King Harald of Norway, Queen Beatrix of the Netherlands and Prince Phillipe of Belgium, Queen Sylvia of Sweden, Mrs Laura Bush of the United States, King Gustav of Sweden, and King Constantine of Greece.

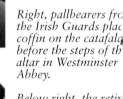

Below, the coffin car[ried] by the bearer party, with the Queen Mot[her's] crown surmounting [it,] moves up the Abbey'[s] centre aisle towards t[he] catafalque in the Lan[tern.]

Right, pallbearers fro[m] the Irish Guards plac[e the] coffin on the catafal[que] before the steps of th[e] altar in Westminster Abbey.

Below right, the retir[ing] procession moves bac[k] down the aisle at the conclusion of the ser[vice] following the soundi[ng] of The Last Post and Reveille, and the sing[ing] of the National Anth[em.]

visibly affected, wiping tears from his eyes as he and other members of the royal family and guests departed. The Prince, who had flown back from Klosters on the Saturday, had subsequently given a personal account of how much the Queen Mother had meant to him in a brief television tribute, saying that she was "simply the most magical grandmother you could possibly have, and I was utterly devoted to her. For me she meant everything and I had dreaded, dreaded this moment. Somehow I never thought it would come. She seemed gloriously unstoppable."

His two sons added their own memories shortly after Friday's procession, recalling in particular her sense of humour. "Every single thing that went wrong or was funny for any reason," Prince William said, "she laughed herself stupid about. It kept us all sane." Prince Harry added that his great-grandmother had been an inspiration. "She was amazing, and she was very interested in everything we did."

As the guests departed from Westminster Hall, members of the public began to file through, and it rapidly became evident that the number of people wanting to do so was far greater than had been expected. As the queues stretched back across Lambeth Bridge and some miles along the south bank of the river, the hall had to be kept open throughout most of the night hours from Friday to Monday, in spite of the intense cold, and by the time the doors finally closed on Tuesday morning, it was estimated that more than 200,000 people had passed by the coffin. Those who came on the final evening will have seen the four grandsons—the Prince of Wales, the Duke of York, the Earl of Wessex and Viscount Linley—replace the guards at the four corners of the catafalque and stand, with heads bowed, silent and immobile for 20 minutes. The Prince of Wales returned later in the night to stand quietly looking at the coffin for a further 20 minutes.

The crowds gathering in Parliament Square and outside Westminster Abbey on the morning of the funeral heard the Abbey's great tenor bell toll once a minute for 101 minutes, reflecting the years of the Queen Mother's life, as the coffin was moved from Westminster Hall to the magnificence of Westminster Abbey for the funeral service. It was a setting the Queen Mother knew well. She was married to Prince Albert here in 1923, was crowned beside him at the coronation in 1937, attended her daughter's coronation in 1953 and was present at many other royal occasions in the Abbey.

The congregation of more than 2,000 attending the service was led by the Queen and other members of the royal family as well as a substantial gathering of representatives from other monarchies, including the Queen of the Netherlands, the King and Prince Philippe of Belgium, the Sultan of Brunei, the Queen and Prince Consort of Denmark, Prince Gustav of Sayn-Wittgenstein-Berleburg, the King and Queen of Sweden, the King and Queen of Spain, the King and Queen of Norway, King Michael and Queen Ana of Romania, King Constantine and Queen Anne-Marie of the Hellenes, the Grand Duke and Grand

" STRENGTH, DIGNITY AND LAUGHTER ARE THE THREE GREAT GIFTS WHICH WE HONOUR AND CELEBRATE TODAY. "

Duchess of Luxembourg, Prince Albert of Monaco, Princess Muna of Jordan, Prince and Princess Ernst-August of Hanover, Prince Hans-Adam of Liechtenstein and the Duke of Aosta.

The congregation also included many leading British politicians, including the Prime Minister and his four surviving predecessors—Lord Callaghan, Sir Edward Heath, Lady Thatcher and Mr John Major—as well as representatives of foreign countries, including Mrs Laura Bush, wife of the President of the United States. Many relatives of the Queen Mother, members of her staff, representatives of the charities she supported during the last 80 years, and long-standing friends, such as Dame Vera Lynn, Sir John Mills and the writer and jockey Dick Francis, were also present.

During the service two of the Queen Mother's favourite hymns were sung, "Immortal, Invisible, God only wise" and "Guide Me, O thou great Redeemer", not just by the choir and congregation within the Abbey, but also by many of the crowd gathered outside its walls. Lessons were read by the Archbishop of York, Dr David Hope, and by Cardinal Cormac Murphy-O'Connor, the Archbishop of Westminster, and the sermon was preached by the Archbishop of Canterbury, Dr George Carey, who spoke of the Queen Mother bathing us, like the sun, "with her warm glow". He drew from the book of Proverbs a description of a gracious woman, which read: "Strength and dignity are her clothing and she laughs at the time to come." Strength, dignity and laughter, the Archbishop said, were the "three great gifts which we honour and celebrate today".

It was a theme that had resounded in many of the countless tributes paid to the Queen Mother in the 10 days following her death, and not just in such formal surroundings as Westminster Abbey. This popular recognition of her qualities was made evident again, and finally, as the service ended and the coffin emerged from the Abbey, to the accompaniment of a half-muffled peal of the bells. As the coffin was transferred to a limousine for the last journey to Windsor, accompanied by Prince Charles in a following car, people were found to be lining the route all the way to bid a last public farewell as the coffin was taken through the gates to St George's Chapel in Windsor Castle, where the Queen Mother was later buried alongside her husband, and her King.

The Queen, in a televised broadcast on the eve of her mother's funeral, said that she had been deeply moved by the outpouring of affection that had accompanied her death. "The extent of the tribute that huge numbers of you have paid to my mother in the last few days has been overwhelming," she said, adding that she hoped the sadness of the following day's ceremony would "blend with a wider sense of thanksgiving". Queen Elizabeth the Queen Mother herself said, near the end of her life, that it had been her "joy and privilege to serve this dear land and its people". The reaction to her death showed that the joy and privilege had been more than shared by the land and its people. ■

Above, the funeral car leaves Westminster on its journey towards The Mall and thence along the A4 to Windsor. It was estimated that more than a million people lined the route of the funeral procession.

Left, some in the crowd had been camping overnight to secure good vantage points on and around Parliament Square.

Right, the captains and the kings, politicians and other dignitaries depart via the Abbey's west door.

Above, the massed pipes and drums led the procession to the Abbey and played a lament as the coffin departed.

Left, an old soldier remembers what many have forgotten, or never knew.

Top right, following the service, a Battle of Britain memorial flight of two Spitfires and a Lancaster bomber flew over Buckingham Palace.

Right, the funeral car approaches its final destination in Windsor.

" IT HAS BEEN MY JOY AND PRIVILEGE TO SERVE THIS DEAR LAND AND ITS PEOPLE. "

For The Illustrated London News: Text by Margaret Laing; Editor James Bishop. Lisa Barnard, Alison Booth, Sarah Carrington, Jeanette Collins, Margaret Davies, Rosemary Duffy, Nathan Eaton-Baudains, Fiona Ferguson, Elaine Hart, Adrian Hulf, Pete Kraushaar, Adrianne LeMan, Liz Moore, Suzanne Pavely, Linda Phillips, Richard Pitkin, Tony Price, Susie Rowbottom, Tracey Vosvenieks, John Webster.

PICTURE CREDITS

Front cover, Camera Press. 6, Queen Victoria/Hulton Deutsch Collection; Prince Albert/Bridgeman Art Library; Edward VII and Alexandra/Popperfoto; Princes of Wales/ET Archive. 7, George VI and family/Camera Press; Annigoni portrait of the Queen/Bridgeman Art Library; Prince of Wales and family/Camera Press. 8, portrait of Lady Elizabeth Bowes-Lyon/Lord Chamberlain. 17, boy scout/Adrianne LeMan. 21, Queen Mother with soldier/Syndication Int. 25, leaving Palace/Popperfoto. 28, Queen Mother, top right/Photo Source. 32-3, General Strike/BBC Hulton Picture Library. 33, Al Jolson/National Film Archives. 34, Sydney Bridge/Susan Griggs. 34-5, Reichstag fire/Popperfoto. 35, Mao Tse-Tung/Popperfoto; Piccadilly Circus/Photo Source. 36-7, Silver Jubilee painting/Bridgeman Art Library. 38, Jesse Owens/Sport & General. 39, Abdication placards/Norman Parkinson; Queen Mother and family, Camera Press. 40, Portrait of Queen Elizabeth by Gerald Kelly, National Portrait Gallery. 42, "Queen Mary" launch/Photo Source. 43, portrait, centre/Camera Press; portrait, top right/Photo Source; Inspection/Photo Source. 44, Queen Mother with bouquet/Press Association. 45, Queen Mother & Prince Charles/Camera Press; at funeral of George VI/Photo Source. 48, "Guernica"/DACS/Prado. 50, Heinkel HE178/Popperfoto; in Montreal/Sport & General. 51, Germany invades Poland/Popperfoto. 53, Warsaw ghetto/Popperfoto; El Alamein/Popperfoto. 54, Paris liberated/Photo Source. 55, VE Day, Piccadilly Circus/BBC Hulton Picture Library; Hiroshima/BBC Hulton Picture Library/Bettmann. 56-7, Queen & Duke of Edinburgh at their wedding/Camera Press. 56, Mountbatten/Popperfoto; Land-Rover/J Harvey. 58, christening/Press Association; Dan Archer/BBC Radio; Festival of Britain/BBC Hulton Picture Library; Burgess/Popperfoto; Maclean/Popperfoto; last tram/London Regional Transport. 59, Festival of Britain/Photo Source; "The Mousetrap"/Mander & Mitchenson. 62, Queen Mother with corgi/Camera Press; Queen Mother in tiara/Photo Source. 63, Queen Mother/Tim Graham. 65, Queen Mother/Tim Graham. 66, Coronation robes, 1953/Associated Press; on balcony/Press Association. 67, Queen & Duke of Edinburgh/Camera Press. 68, Hillary & Tenzing/Times (London). 69, "Flying Bedstead"/Popperfoto; in Southern Rhodesia/Camera Press; at Windsor Castle/BBC Hulton Picture Library. 70, at Biggin Hill/Photo Source; Premium Bond/J Harvey/Lizard; Calder Hall/Topham. 71, hovercraft/Press Association; Hungarian uprising/BBC Hulton Picture Library. 72, Krushchev/Camera Press; B Russell/Popperfoto; in New South Wales/Camera Press; at Surf Carnival/Photo Source. 73, Cuba poster/Topham; at British Embassy/Photo Source; at Vatican/Topham. 74, Morris Mini-Minor/National Motor Museum; Motorway/Topham; traffic warden/BBC Hulton Picture Library. 74-5, wedding/Camera Press. 75, 'My Spy Flight'/John Frost; Khrushchev at UN/Topham. 76, betting shops/Topham. 76-7, Cuba blockade/John Frost. 77, M Monroe/Rex Features; Y Gagarin & V Vladimirovna/Science Photo Library; Eichmann/Popperfoto. 78, portrait/Camera Press. 79, assassination/Popperfoto; Queen Mother, Lord Snowdon & Princess Margaret/Photo Source. 80, Beatles/Rex; Queen Mother at Ideal Home Exhibition/Photo Source. 80-1, World Cup 1966/Gerry Cranham; Aberfan 1966/Popperfoto; Queen at Aberfan/Topham. 82, Queen Mother at Sandown/Syndication International; F Chichester/Camera Press; Luther King march/Popperfoto. 83, King, inset/Popperfoto; at unveiling of plaque/Photo Source; with Gloucester/Photo Source; at Braemar Gathering/Photo Source. 84, man on moon/ZEFA. 85, Concorde/Popperfoto; Prince Charles' investiture/Press Association. 86, Soyuz ll/Associated Press. 86-7, royal family/Camera Press. 87, Mark Spitz/Allsport. 89, Flixborough/Photo Source; Haile Selassie/Rex; President Nixon/Rex; Queen Mother and Queen at dog trials/Photo Source; at Royal College of Music/Photo Source. 90, Norman Parkinson portrait/Camera Press; Juan Carlos and Franco/Rex; North Sea oil/Rex. 91, Soyuz and Apollo dock/Associated Press; Mars/NASA. 93, Elvis/Rex; Naomi James/Topham; Louise

Brown/Rex; Queen Mother & Princess Margaret/Tim Graham. 94, Thatcher/Tim Graham; US helicopter Iran/Rex; Iranian Embassy, London/Rex; Borg/Leo Mason; Lennon & Yoko/Rex. 94-5, Queen Mother and corgi/Camera Press. 95, Queen Mother, Queen and Princess Margaret/Camera Press/Norman Parkinson; outside Clarence House/Tim Graham; at opera/Tim Graham; with Prince Charles/Tim Graham. 96, Princess Alice/Camera Press; SDP/Camera Press; London Marathon/Allsport; Charles and Diana kiss/Tim Graham; Columbia shuttle/Rex. 97, Charles and Diana wedding/Rex; Zara's christening/Camera Press; William's christening/Press Association; Queen Mother at 82/Tim Graham. 98, America's Cup/Leo Mason; Yvonne Fletcher/UPITN; York Minster ablaze/Press Agency (Yorkshire) Ltd; Queen Mother on Concorde/Tim Graham. 99, christening/Camera Press. 100, wedding/Tim Graham; Queen/Camera Press; hurricane/Ed Pritchard; Challenger/Sipa. 101, Hillsborough/Gamma; Maradona/Bob Thomas; Lockerbie, Herald of Free Enterprise/Corbis Sygma. 102, Tiananmen/Magnum; Wall/Katz; Thatcher resigns/Syndication Int; Mary Robinson/Spooner; Queen in Malaysia/Photographers Int. 103, Queen Mother portrait/Camera Press; Queen Mother at Palladium, birthday greetings/Tim Graham; WVS float, Children's Society float/Alpha; fireworks/Rex. 104, Gandhi funeral/J McCarthy/Corbis Sygma; Soyuz/Rex; Queen & President Bush/Photographers Int. 105, tank Gulf War/Magnum; US troops Kuwait/Corbis Sygma; T Waite/Press Association. 106, Sir Ranulph Fiennes/Corbis Sygma; Prince & Princess of Wales, Windsor fire/Rex; Waco fire/Corbis Sygma; L Christie, S Gunnel/Allsport. 107, R Stephens, B Boothroyd/Rex; Queen Mother at Elizabeth Gate/Tim Graham; ordination of women/Corbis Sygma; Nureyev/Camera Press. 108, Channel Tunnel opening/Anwar Hussein; Blair/Rex; lottery, Australian bush fire/Corbis Sygma; Mandela/Gamma; World Cup/Empics. 109, Queen in South Africa/Photographers Int; Queen Mother 95th/Corbis Sygma; VE-Day Buckingham Palace, Red Arrows/Rex; OJ Simpson/Corbis Sygma; N Leeson/Camera Press. 110, Skye bridge/Rex; Diana/Camera Press; Dunblane wreaths, Fenice/Corbis Sygma. 111, Sea Empress, Arndale centre/Rex; Queen in Thailand/Camera Press; D Bailey at Olympics/Gamma. 112, Diana/Corbis Sygma; Blair/Camera Press; Tiger Woods/Gamma; Dolly the sheep/Rex; Louise Woodward/Rex; Hong Kong handover/Magnum. 113, Diana/Gamma; Diana with halo/Tim Graham; floral tributes, Diana's funeral/Camera Press; Elton John/Rex. 114, Clinton/Rex; Beckham/Allsport; Sinatra/Rex; the euro/Corbis Sygma; Queen Mother/Solo; Irish Assembly/PA Photos. 115, Omagh/Corbis Sygma; royal wedding/Rex; Turkish earthquake/Corbis Sygma; eclipse/PA Photos; demo/Rex. 116, Concorde/Popperfoto; Adams, Putin, Kursk, Redgrave, May Day/PA Photos. 117, Blair baby, Livingstone/PA Photos; Venus Williams/Rex; Queen Mother in Scotland/JS Library International. 118, Queen Mother in carriage, at St Paul's, with the Queen/Camera Press; Royal Family on balcony/Alpha; Red Arrows/Aviation Images. 119, corgis, Buckingham Palace, Queen Mother at St Paul's, Wombles/Camera Press. 120, New York/Getty; President Bush/Rex; Afghanistan/PA Photos. 121, Margaret's funeral/Camera Press; Queen Mother at Ark Royal/Rex; Queen and Princess Anne riding/Reuters; Royal Marines, the Queen Mother's coffin/PA Photos. 122-23, The Mall/PA Photos; Prince Charles/Topham/Pressnet; Royal family, close up of Royal family, coffin/Rex; guards marching/Lucy Baker. 124-25, Queen/Reuters; floral tributes, queues along South Bank, inside Westminster Hall, gin bottle/Lucy Baker; guards carrying coffin, catafalque, Princes William and Harry and Princess Anne/PA Photos. 126-27, inside Westminster Abbey, royal family following the coffin, Laura Bush, Dr Carey/PA Photos; crown/Lucy Baker; Queen of Spain, King of Norway, Queen of the Netherlands, Queen of Sweden, King of Sweden, King of Greece/Reuters; parading pipers/Simon Cherry; the Lantern in the Abbey/Tim Rooke/Rex. 128-29, hearse carrying coffin through Parliament Square, hearse at Windsor Castle, Chelsea Pensioner/PA Photos; crowds, pipers/David Reed; Spitfires, Queen/Reuters; mourners outside Abbey/Simon Cherry; Queen Mother/Topham/Pressnet. Back cover, Lord Chamberlain. All other pictures/The Illustrated London News.